Introductions in Feminist Theology

3

Editorial Committee

Mary Grey
Lisa Isherwood
Catherine Norris
Janet Wootton

Sheffield Academic Press

Introducing Thealogy: Discourse on the Goddess

Melissa Raphael

To Michael

Copyright © 1999 Sheffield Academic Press

Published by Sheffield Academic Press Ltd
Mansion House
19 Kingfield Road
Sheffield S11 9AS
England

Printed on acid-free paper in Great Britain
by Cromwell Press
Trowbridge, Wiltshire

British Library Cataloguing in Publication Data

A catalogue record for this book is available
from the British Library

ISBN 1-85075-975-8

Table of Contents

Editor's Preface

The Britain and Ireland School of Feminist Theology was set up with the intention of making the feminist voice in theology accessible to as wide an audience as possible. The 'Introductions' series aims to do this through readable and scholarly books tackling a range of topics from scripture to the body. All are written with the intention of shaking the complacency of the patriarchal discourse in theology, by showing that others ways of doing theology are not only possible but life-enhancing.

Melissa Raphael has written for another BISFT and Sheffield Academic Press project, that of the occasional series and her work *Thealogy and Embodiment: The Post-Patriarchal Reconstruction of Female Sacrality* has received good reviews. It is a stimulating work dealing with the thealogical significance of the female body, and raising many questions and shaking many assumptions.

In this the fourth of the 'Introducing' titles, Melissa Raphael engages with thealogy in a challenging and informative way. Those coming to the discipline for the first time will be introduced to a new way of thinking, while those conversant with the area are asked to look with new eyes at well known material and concepts.

The conversation between theology and thealogy is opening up many areas of profound discomfort on both sides, yet at the same time prompting leaps of insight and political awareness. It is hoped that this book will provide a grounding for those who wish to continue the conversation and further the transformation of the theological map.

Lisa Isherwood and Mary Grey

Acknowledgments

I would like to offer my heartfelt thanks to the editorial team for their support. Thanks are also due to Graham Harvey, Beverley Clack, Ruth Mantin, Wendy Griffin, Michael York, Asphodel Long, Alix Pirani, Paul Bowen, priestess Shân Jayran and many others who together form an academic community sharing research and friendship in the field of Goddess studies. I am also grateful to Vera Roberts for her generous loan of books at an early stage of my research into Goddess feminism, and to all those who have invited me to teach, speak and publish on thealogy, thereby helping to increase awareness of this significant development in the history of women's religion and of religion in the West. Lastly, I would like to express my gratitude to my husband Michael and my young daughter Verity for the great sustenance they have given to this and all my work.

Introduction

When proof-readers and computer spell-checks come across the word 'thealogy' in a text they usually assume it is a typographical error and inadvertently undo two decades of religious feminist theory by changing it back to the masculine 'theology'. It was nearly twenty years ago that the Canadian scholar Naomi Goldenberg first used the term 'thealogy' to denote feminist discourse on *thea* (the Goddess) instead of *theo* (God) (1979: 96; 1987: 37-52). But it seems that outside the religious feminist academy, elements of the Pagan community and Goddess feminist circles themselves, few are as yet familiar with the term. And yet such is the power of language that those who *have* adopted the term have found their world view altered, if not transformed, by the substitution of theology's 'o' for an 'a'. Of course it takes more than a neologism to change people's lives, but in many ways the word 'thealogy' has named, and therefore empowered, a spiritual/political paradigm shift whose effects are not, as yet, fully calculable.

The Purpose of This Book

This book is intended to introduce students, teachers and the general reader to the context and main elements of thealogy—here understood to be not just general discourse on the goddesses of the world's religions, but as a contemporary feminist discourse on the divine, here identified as 'the Goddess'.[1] Through its notes and references the book is also intended to launch the reader into a growing body of writing on the Goddess. To date, most of the books that have been written about the Goddess and the rituals that celebrate her have been intended for a

---

1.   Technical terms are not the sole property of those who first use them. I am open to the suggestion that 'thealogy' could refer to any sort of discourse on any sort of goddess. I have chosen, however, to make some sort of feminist claim to the term as it appeared to originate in religious feminist discourse and, at present, has widest currency among Goddess feminists.

non-academic audience consisting of those already participant in the Goddess movement. It now seems necessary to provide students and others with a relatively concise introduction to those participant texts (for which this book is not a substitute).

In his recent book *Listening People, Speaking Earth*, Graham Harvey was quite right to point out that the Goddess movement 'is not all about books or about reading, writing, studying, thinking, discussing. It is also concerned with living life' (1997: 77). Although the experience thealogy is grounded in cannot be, and has not been, ignored, it will be noted that the present study is entitled *Introducing Thealogy*, not *Goddess Religion*. Despite this introduction's sketch of the contemporary Goddess movement and my intention to keep the whole study contextually grounded, this book is not an empirical study of the feminist wing of the Goddess movement. Rather, it is an exposition of a body of thought—thealogy—that derives from Goddess women's experience and from a broader history of emancipatory ideas and which can be defined as feminist reflection on the femaleness of the divine and the divinity of femaleness,[2] and, more generally, spiritual, ethical and political reflection on the meaning(s) of both.

To write an introductory overview of thealogy is not, perhaps, at present, a very thealogical thing to do. The word 'thealogy' might indicate that the Goddess is the object of a reasoned discourse; a discipline comparable to theology as reasoned discourse on God. However, that is usually far from the case. Thealogy is not founded upon a body of authoritative and sacred texts. Although writers like Carol Christ, Monica Sjöö, Starhawk, Naomi Goldenberg and (differently) Mary Daly have all reflected on the religious and political ramifications of celebrating female divinity, thealogizing is not an intellectual project that many Goddess feminists undertake for its own sake. Most do not so much theorize the Goddess as experience her more immediately in themselves and in the natural environment. For example, in their

2.   Charlotte Caron defines thealogy in a similar way as 'reflection on the divine in feminine and feminist terms' (1996: 281). However, not all Goddess feminists would be content with the use of the word 'feminine' in this context. The concept of the Goddess may be feminine rather than masculine in character, but she is in no sense an incarnation of femininity as envisaged by patriarchally prescribed virtues for women such as meekness, humility, silence, passivity and so forth. For these reasons, most Goddess feminists avoid the word 'feminine' and prefer to use the less sentimental, less idealizing, words 'female' and 'femaleness'.

different ways, the performance artists Carolyn Hillyer in Dartmoor and
Jill Smith in the Western Isles experience nature (her)itself as a comprehensive thealogical text. They find and know—or better—*inhabit* the
Goddess in the wild, untamed landscape. Their painting and poetry are
inspired by the memory and form of the Goddess in the landscape.
Indeed, for Jill Smith the very island of Britain is the body of the Goddess lying in the sea.[3]

Moreover, for many Goddess feminists, to theorize thealogically might
be to adopt the kind of disembodied, elitist God(dess)'s-eye-view on the
world that has been so characteristic of patriarchal scholarship. It has,
after all, become a commonplace of religious feminism that feminist
theo/alogical method should move from experience to concepts, rather
than beginning with abstract and acontextual theory that is unrelated to,
or brackets out, real injustices and real experiences. Goddess women
generally prefer to take their own path in and to the Goddess; she makes
a practical and experiential, not merely conceptual, difference. For that
reason, not everyone in the Goddess movement would be comfortable
with the term 'thealogy' or would welcome the assimilation of their
spirituality into an academic discipline (See Raphael 1996b; Long 1996;
MacIntyre 1996). Perhaps only a minority of Goddess feminists would
appreciate the form, voice and method of Carol Christ's newly published 'systematic thealogy', *Rebirth of the Goddess*. (Although Christ's
book is experientially grounded it nonetheless has a structure which
consciously replicates that of traditional systematic theology [1997: xv].)

In the light of these observations, it might seem surprising that I
should believe that a full-length exposition of thealogy would be of
benefit to its readers. But I hope that it will be so for several reasons.
First, it seems to me that concepts and experiences are interpenetrated as
one process of living and knowing. We cannot *have* experiences without
the concepts that identify and accommodate those experiences as relevant and meaningful. Conversely, a conceptual frame develops in the
process of making sense of experience. Thealogy is, therefore, inherent
in Goddess feminism precisely *as* a lived religion and its articulation
helps to clarify and focus that lived experience as well as explain and
recommend it to other women.

Secondly, there is an issue of intellectual integrity involved. Goddess
feminism is in many ways a child of modern rationalism and should

3.   Slide show, 'Goddess Mountains of the Western Isles' given at the 1997 Goddess Conference, Glastonbury, 9 August 1997.

be proud of its parentage: the Enlightenment and the emancipatory movements of liberal humanism, Marxism and feminism itself that it generated (Grigg 1995: 87). Goddess feminism is rightly critical of the abstracted qualities of masculinist rationalism and rightly insists that talk about the Goddess grows or repatterns organically in ways akin to the Goddess/nature herself. It is questionable whether it is appropriate to reify thealogy almost as if it were an intellectual project like any other. Yet Goddess feminism is, nonetheless, quite clearly informed by religious, philosophical and political concepts and ideas which are as available to exposition as those of any other religious world view. I would strongly agree with Carol Christ that 'thea-logy [sic] as a whole can be seen to be governed by an internal logic and a number of basic insights' (1997: xv). Without turning thealogy into a 'discipline' with all the dreariness and sublimated violence that word connotes, there seems to be a degree of consensus and common affirmation within texts and among Goddess women such that one can say that thealogy does exist as a body of discourse, that given concepts are characteristic of thealogy and that, like other discourses that envision a just and peace-loving future, it can serve a profoundly liberative purpose.

Thirdly, following the 'Ambivalent Goddesses' conference held at King Alfred's College, Winchester in 1997—one of the first conferences of its kind in Britain—a new field called Goddess Studies has begun to develop within the British academy and includes, among others, anthropological, historical and thealogical approaches to the study of the Goddess in ancient and contemporary non-feminist Paganism, and in Pagan and non-Pagan Goddess feminism. This book is intended to contribute to the further development of Goddess Studies as an area of scholarship that breaks with patriarchal tradition and, at last, views goddesses and the Goddess as being of more than peripheral interest to religious people and to the study of religion.

Moreover, the development of thealogy as an academic discourse and as an object of analysis does not seem to me to have alienated or appropriated thealogy from Goddess women. Indeed, it probably serves the thealogical cause since, even without teachers intending to change the lives of students, higher and continuing educational programmes offering courses on the history and revival of Goddess religion often inspire women to become involved with Goddess feminism or to incorporate the Goddess into their own spirituality (See Harvey 1997: 78; 1993: 10-13).

Questions of Method

Although thealogy is now being taught in the academy, the reader will not find summaries of the work of 'key' thealogians in the present study, in the way that she or he might in an introduction to, say, modern theology. Although a writer/practitioner may have particular emphases, thealogians do not take a 'line' and then claim it as their own. Thealogy is not constituted by the work of authoritative theoreticians whose work must be 'mastered' and sycophantically applied. Consequently, quotation within the present study does not discriminate between those who write thealogy from an academic background and those who do not. This is because, metaphorically speaking, thealogy is an open, egalitarian web, not a locked tower from whose windows one or two are privileged to speak on behalf of the multitude listening below. Thealogical texts are interconnected and in continual non-hierarchical conversation. Bearing this in mind, rather than homogenize thealogical voices, I have tried wherever possible to let Goddess feminists speak for themselves. While an introduction to a body or process of thought must, by its nature, generalize, I have endeavoured to note important differences and shifts of opinion within this still fluid, emergent movement.

Two further methodological points should be made. First, it might appear that this book uses the phrase 'the Goddess' as if everyone meant the same thing by it. That this not the case will become apparent in the second chapter of this study. For some, the Goddess is not *the* Goddess, but simply (and more abstractly) 'Goddess'. For others, 'the Goddess' sounds too monotheistic—too like a feminized God—and they prefer to speak polytheistically of Goddesses. For some the Goddess is a real self-originating divinity in her own right; for others, who might consider themselves atheists, she is a liberating archetype whose power is psychological and political rather than external to and transcendent of the individual or movement. Others again will move freely between a number of positions.

This open texture of thealogical discussion is not a mark of intellectual laxity but belongs to a world view that recognizes that knowledge does not stand over and against the individual as dogma 'out there', but is embodied and lived and therefore shifts with mood and time. So although, for simplicity's sake, this study refers to the Goddess, as most Goddess feminists do, in a basically monotheistic style, I have not established any normative concept of the Goddess, but have rather let my sources shape her meaning(s) in ways relevant to them and to the context. It will also be noted that when I refer to the Goddess as a distinct contemporary feminist conception of the divine I capitalize her name; when referring to ancient and contemporary goddesses in general, I do not. The lack of a capital letter is intended to differentiate between the general and the specific, not to denigrate the former.

Secondly, exposition is not necessarily dispassionate and this book's exposition of thealogy makes no pretence of being so. Its contents have been shaped in several interrelated ways: namely, by my responses to the recurrent questions students ask in class about thealogy and Goddess feminism, by my interpretation of Goddess texts, events and discussions with Goddess women, and by the filtering of these through the lens of my own identity as a Jewish feminist. My practice of Judaism and my sense of Jewishness have been radically reconfigured by feminism and by the work of some Jewish feminists in reclaiming the Jewish goddess heritage for women today. While this does not make me a Goddess religionist or a Pagan, it means that Goddess religion is more for me than a mere object of examination. This book may be intended to inform rather than persuade, but I hope that reading it will prove more than an exercise in intellectual tourism. One does not have to be a Goddess religionist to find in the Goddess

> a compelling image of female power, a vision of the deep connection of all beings in the web of life, and a call to create peace on earth. The return of the Goddess inspires us to hope that we can heal the deep rifts between women and men, between "man" and nature, and between "God" and the world, that have shaped our western view of reality for far too long (Christ 1997: xiii).

Goddess Feminism as a New/Old Religion

The origins of Goddess feminism can be traced through a history of modern, emancipatory ideas and movements. From the late seventeenth century through to the early nineteenth century, Enlightenment and Romantic criticism of governmental institutions like the Church and the monarchy was to inform egalitarian, anti-authoritarian arguments for the independence of human reason from faith and, among the radical foremothers and forefathers of Goddess feminists, for the essential equality and dignity of persons regardless of race, gender, property and class. In the nineteenth century Christian feminism was also to pave the way

for contemporary religious feminism by challenging the prevailing ideology of femininity that kept women out of the public religious sphere.
Then in the 1960s and 70s, through both the taboo-breaking rebellious-
ness of the counterculture and the socio-religious criticism advanced by
the Women's Liberation movement, women were empowered with a
sense that, as sisters, they could overturn patriarchal institutions. From
the mid-1970s onwards, women's recognition that they could break
away from the biblical feminist project without relinquishing religion
and spirituality altogether was to culminate in the birth of a new political stratagem and a new religion or spirituality: Goddess feminism.

Commentators are agreed that Goddess religion is increasing in numbers of adherents and in influence in America, Europe and Australasia.
For those who want it to, Goddess religion can now constitute an alternative religion that is nonetheless comparable with other religions. Cynthia Eller has argued that Goddess feminism in America is 'creating a
new religion in our time' because it quite clearly fulfils the criteria by
which religion is commonly defined, namely, it relates to the sacred or
numinous in practical, social and mythological ways (1993: 39). Where
Goddess feminism celebrates its own divinity—the Goddess or Great
Mother—its own rituals for purification, healing and psychological
empowerment, seasonal festivals relating to the Pagan 'wheel of the
year', rites of initiation and passage (as at menarche and menopause), a
priesthood, a sacred history, mythology, symbology, thealogy, and
sacred sites, it can be said to constitute either a variant type of contemporary Pagan religion or a politically and institutionally independent
women's religion.

A religion gives its practitioners a particular orientation of consciousness. In this sense too one can justify calling Goddess feminism a
religion rather than a spirituality when the Goddess becomes the very
heart and centre of a woman or man's being; that is, when the Goddess
becomes what Richard Grigg calls 'the transformative relationship
between self and nature, the power of being, and other selves' (1995:
52). When Carol Christ defines the Goddess as nothing less than 'the
power of intelligent embodied love that is the ground of all being'; a
power of reconnection that returns or binds us back to our connections
with the web of life, she renders Goddess feminism almost definitively a
religion, as the Indo-European roots of the word 'religion' are *re*, *leig*: to
bind or turn back (1997: xv-xvi).

However, not everyone in the Goddess movement would welcome the assimilation of their spiritual practices and politics into a something that sounds as institutionalized and conventional as a religion. There are mixed responses to the notion of Goddess feminism as a religion. 'Religion' is, for many, a highly ambivalent term connoting all the dogmatic, expansionist and authoritarian characteristics of institutionalized patriarchal religion. As Donate Pahnke notes, in order to distance themselves from such negative aspects of religion, some Goddess feminists prefer to see their practices as constituting a spirituality rather than a religion. Others (in Germany at least) resist patriarchy's misappropriation of the religious impulse and regard their practices as *authentic* religion (Pahnke 1995: 167-72).

Whatever status Goddess feminism is ascribed, it must be remembered that not everyone who celebrates the Goddess has left their church or synagogue and, therefore, invocation of the Goddess does not always indicate the presence of a new and separate religion. Some of the more radical Christian and Jewish feminist theology may blend at the edges with thealogy (especially where Goddess imagery is used to evoke the divine). Nonetheless, most thealogy is not just a differently nuanced feminist theology. Thealogy is a feminist discourse predominantly emergent from a distinct Goddess movement which has its own journals and organizes its own events for the celebration of the Goddess and the sharing of insight and experience.[4] As Shân Jayran writes (1997), 'Now that Western Goddess religion is growing in numbers and sophistication, away from an earlier, scattered, isolated and marginal standing, it must negotiate its place among other goddess religions worldwide.' Here the recovery of the Goddess signals the rebirth of a pre-biblical religion or spirituality perceived by Goddess women to be archaic and native to all parts of the world. And here, in its contemporary feminist form, the Goddess is at the centre of the religion; not merely an aspect of a religion or an attribute of divinity subordinated to 'higher' male attributes.

In short, this study agrees with those scholars who argue that Goddess feminism can, though not always does, constitute a religion, but does not assume that thealogy will inform any one institutional context. In fact, Goddess feminists have not been inclined to set up church, sect or

---

4.　For example, spiritual feminism is prevalent in the women's peace camps at Greenham, Menwith Hill U.S. surveillance base (known to radical feminists as the Womenwith [sic] Women's Peace Camp), Sellafield nuclear reprocessing plant and Aldermaston where British nuclear weapons are manufactured.

cult-type institutions to rival those they have rejected. (Indeed, a 'feminist Goddess cult' would be something of an oxymoron as Goddess religion is without a single founder, a charismatic leadership, hierarchy, coercion or any notions of obedience to authority.)

However, when Goddess feminism *is* pursued on a more formal basis as an organized women's religion, ordination programmes for priestesses and other such formal religious phenomena may be established. For example, in the United States, the Re-formed Congregation of the Goddess has been established by Jade and other lesbian feminist witches. Out of the (women only) Re-formed Congregation of the Goddess has come the Women's Thealogical Institute which offers a training leading to legal ministerial status and credentials. The Institute has, according to Jade, one of its founders, 'designed one of the first leadership development programs for Goddess women since the fall of the great temples. It was important to us [its founders] that this course of study reflects the values that had grown out of the feminist movement.' The Institute offers six categories of study, known as 'the Cella Paths'. These are structured to serve each practitioner's needs and interests. The paths include that of Creatrix, Earthwalker, Scholar/Teacher, Ritualist, Healer and Organizer, each enabling women to celebrate and serve the Goddess in distinctive ways. The Creatrix celebrates the Goddess through art, drama, writing and other exercises of the imagination; the Earthwalker through more practical activities; the Scholar through sharing her research into the Goddess; the Ritualist through creating and adapting rituals; the Healer by giving others the means to sustain their own health, and the Organizer through setting up public events that enable others to share in the energy of the Goddess. After completing these paths of study a woman is certified a priestess: a 'Mistress of Wicca'. Priestesses who 'have learned to walk their own paths to the Goddess will be able to assist others, each woman showing a way for others to celebrate and serve the Goddess'. The Mistress of Wicca is 'an advanced practitioner, not unlike a member of the clergy in other religions' (Jade 1995: 81–82).

That said, students of Goddess feminism will not, on the whole, find contemporary temples built for the Goddess as one would find them built for the divinities of other traditions. Although Mimi Lobell produced a remarkable design for a temple to the Goddess in 1975, it has not, to my knowledge, been built. Lobell's plan for the temple is one in which the building is itself a spiralling, labyrinthine, web-like image of the Goddess; with a spring bubbling forth in the very centre of the labyrinth and the domed ceiling depicting the twenty-four phases of the moon (Göttner-Abendroth 1991: 113-14). It would not be merely economic considerations that stopped Goddess women from building that sort of great temple to the Goddess. They are unlikely to feel the need of such a building because they are accustomed to making an altar or shrine to the Goddess in their own homes which reflects their own personality and individual spiritual needs. In any case, the Goddess is immanent in the natural environment and in women's own bodies; she does not need to be invoked and mediated in specially sanctified places. In Goddess feminism, the female body is sacred; it incarnates the Goddess to such a degree that sacred space is simply that which the body's being-there sacralizes. There is, therefore, no need of a formal boundary of brick or stone to separate the sacred from the profane.

It may be that some of the reasons most Pagans are unwilling to establish sacred buildings obtain for Goddess feminists as well. Shân Jayran notes that while some Pagans 'dream of having a public Temple' as a focus for the community, it 'would inevitably bring an unwelcome control and influence by those who were the caretakers of such a Temple' (1994: 13). For Goddess feminists too, to erect imposing religious buildings might be to institutionalize; to establish a hierarchy and a tradition and, thereby, to risk the loss of spontaneity, freedom and equality. This would be too high a price for the signalling of a new religious presence in Western society.

Goddess religion and spirituality would not want to be positioned in such a way as to break its connections to other traditions. As I have indicated, some on the alternative fringes of Christian and Jewish communities seek to transform their own religion and spirituality by incorporating the Goddess into the (reclaimed) theology, ritual and liturgy of the tradition. So although Goddess feminism has a distinctive spiritual/ political stamp, emphasizing emancipatory politics and the sacrality of female embodiment, it can also be understood as something of a composite religion which draws upon those parts of other religions which are considered empowering to women or which already honour female divinities (see Eller 1993: 62-82). (As nearly all the world's religions have borrowed and incorporated parts of others, that does not disqualify Goddess feminism from the status of a religion in itself [Eller 1993: 74-82].) Goddesses are, and have been, worshipped throughout the world (albeit in patriarchal contexts and without empowering women politically) (See Billington and Green 1996). Contemporary feminist Goddess religion both takes its place among these traditions and is also far from identical with the indigenous worship of goddesses within a pantheon of gods and goddesses in patriarchal societies. Most Goddess feminists would claim that their religion originates from the prehistoric and ancient world and can be traced to and beyond the mediaeval period when, during the witch craze, Goddess worship went underground because of the persecution and murder of the women who honoured her by the Catholic and Protestant churches.

Despite its claim to continuity with religions of the past and with contemporary goddess religions around the world, Western Goddess religion and thealogy incorporate a wide range of cultural, religious, political and personal migrations and coalitions. Even where some of its themes and motifs are ancient, they are blended and fused in such a way as to render the whole a peculiarly late twentieth-century phenomenon. As I will discuss in more detail in Chapter 1 of this study, contemporary Goddess feminism is an eclectic, politically driven, complex of traditions which adopts and adapts indigenous Pagan practices and makes them its own. A common example of this might be that of the Native American Moon Lodge where spiritual feminists both follow Native American tradition and adapt it to their own needs by using the Moon Lodge as a sacred space for menstruating women to retreat and celebrate their 'blood power'. Numerous elements of numerous traditions inform this new women's tradition and include the mythologies of ancient Northern and Southern Paganisms, the yoga and meditation techniques of Buddhism and Hinduism, Chinese divination and healing techniques such as the *I Ching* and acupuncture, theories of reincarnation loosely derived from the Indian religions, esoteric and folk Judaism and Christianity,[5] and Santería and Vodou.[6]

5.   Although the biblical female divinities Hochmah/Sophia/Wisdom, Shekhinah and Mary do figure in some spiritual feminists' invocations, central biblical symbols, narratives and ritual practices are not prominent in the practices of Goddess feminists (other than for those who have incorporated the Goddess into their Christianity or Judaism). For post-biblical feminists, though, the motifs of the biblical tradition, even female ones, may feel too closely associated with the faith communities they have left behind (See Eller 1993: 73-74). According to the American ethnologist, Wendy Griffin, the goddesses associated with the Jewish tradition are far more commonly invoked (by Jewish and non-Jewish Goddess women) than those associated with the Christian tradition. (Private conversation.)

6.   Santería is a religion of African (Yoruba) origin and incorporates elements of

It is clear that, despite drawing on both Eastern and Western traditions, Goddess feminism is a primarily Western phenomenon. Most Goddess women perceive themselves to be exiles from the Western biblical tradition or from an essentially biblical culture and are united by grief and anger at the way Judaism, Christianity and Islam have suppressed and supplanted the Goddess traditions. As we will see in Chapter 3, Goddess women have a strong sense of loss; a sense that the world's religious history has gone profoundly wrong. Thealogical poetics mourn a world that could have been otherwise:

> The Goddess, who blessed sexual love, whose mystery was revered in each sprouting shoot, was gone. In Her place stood a grass-widower God presiding over a sterile creation (Moorey 1997: 3).

The Size and Composition of the Feminist Wing of the Goddess Movement

Well over a decade ago Margot Adler wrote that, 'the women's spirituality movement is now so large and indefinable that it is like an ocean whose waves push against all shores' (1986: 227). This makes it difficult to give a precise number of Goddess women and men in the world today. Carol Christ has estimated that 'the figure "hundreds of thousands" is not high if all who have been deeply moved by Goddess images and literature are counted' (1997: 183 n. 2).

She may be right, but for at least three reasons, reliable statistical information on Goddess feminists in Europe and America—and especially their number—is hard to come by. First, it is difficult to build a clear sociological profile of Goddess feminists because of the way in which they (do not) organize themselves. Rather than join institutions, Goddess feminists like to communicate informally, often without wanting to claim a classifiable, countable, single, fixed religious identity; others are loosely allied to ephemeral groups, networks and covens.[7] Goddess feminists are, by self-definition, free spirits and free thinkers

---

Roman Catholicism. Santería was developed in Cuba and was taken to the United States after the 1959 Cuban revolution.

7.   Examples of such networks are the American New England Women's Spirituality/Sistercircle Network and the AfraGoddess Spiritual/Cultural Sistahood Network or, in Britain, the women-only Matriarchy Research and Reclaim Network. For contact with MRRN and other groups associated with Goddess religion, see Jayran (1995).

who would not see any good purpose served by setting up the kind of religious administrations that provide researchers with the statistics they often want. Many Goddess feminists (and particularly feminist witches) are solitary practitioners, often developing their religious or spiritual identity intuitively, through buying books about the Goddess and sub-scribing to spiritual feminist journals (such as, in Britain, *From the Flames*, or in America, the broad sheet *Goddessing*).

Secondly, a scholar's classification of a woman as a Goddess feminist would not always be the one she would have chosen for herself. For example, Jewish and Christian traditionalists might regard those feminists who have 'gone too far' in celebrating the divinity of femaleness as 'heretical' Goddess feminists, when they would see themselves as radical or progressive Christians or Jews who are not heretics but, on the con-trary, have returned to the oldest forms of their tradition. Also, for fem-inist witches (who worship or celebrate the Goddess), both social discrimination and the occult or hidden nature of Wicca itself ensure that they may be reluctant to disclose their religious identity.

Thirdly, it is important to recognize that it can be difficult and often unnecessary to distinguish feminist Goddess religionists from other kinds of Western Goddess religionists. The feminist Goddess movement emerged from the women's movement but it also belongs to a far wider (and still emergent) Western Goddess movement. Not all women and men who invoke the Goddess are self-identified feminists. There are many for whom the Goddess or goddesses are simply pre-eminent in a 'mainstream', that is, non-feminist, Pagan religion that has no special interest in sexual politics. For example, one of the best-known main-stream Pagans writing on the Goddess is Caitlín Matthews—who, whilst far from anti-feminist, resists what she sees as the co-option of the God-dess by feminists or women in general (1989: xii, 6, 11). There are some for whom the return of the Goddess is an element or sign of the dawn-ing of the New Age; and there are some of a primarily Jungian bent for whom the Goddess completes the process of their self-development or quest for 'the feminine'. For men on such a quest, the Goddess is sought to complement and balance their masculinity and so help them to achieve psychic wholeness. Those men and women who use the Goddess to reclaim their 'femininity' or to develop a 'women's' or 'fem-inine' (rather than feminist) spirituality may honour the Goddess without explicitly or predominantly political intentions. There is also a minority of Pagans in the Goddess movement who are hostile to feminism (Harvey 1997: 71).

Leaving this last group aside, in a world of patriarchal religions which deny female divinity, make second-class moral and intellectual citizens of their female adherents, and regard female biology as profane, *any* celebration of the Goddess is likely to imply some sort of feminist element. The majority in the Goddess movement do acknowledge the sexual-political dimension of their religion or spirituality. This book, however, focuses on the work of explicitly feminist Pagans and non-Pagans in the Goddess movement. When I and other commentators use the term 'Goddess feminist' this specifies a woman or man who stands in a direct line of inheritance from those Goddess feminists of the mid- to late-1970s who initiated Goddess religion and spirituality in its present form. A Goddess feminist is one who identifies and opposes patriarchal structures of religious and social power and whose religious practice is not only centred on the Goddess but also supports all women's right of access to the sacred and to autonomous religious self-expression and organization.

So while Goddess feminism can be counted a part of the Goddess movement, its political dynamic marks it out from other elements within the movement. For Goddess feminists, the reinstatement of the Goddess is an affirmation and sign of female spiritual/political power. It marks the renewal of a woman-centred or matrifocal system of values believed to have preceded patriarchy. With the renewal of this value system, the beauty and mysterious generativity of the female body, regardless of size and age, and as a part of that divine female body which is the earth or nature itself, can be celebrated and revered once more. The well-being of bodies becomes a sign of the health of their spiritual, political and ecological environment. In this book I have understood thealogy, then, to be a historically and intrinsically feminist discourse and project—a prophetic attempt to name and reclaim female divinity and to use the power generated by that reclamation to the ends of the single process of personal/spiritual/political transformation.

Goddess Feminism and Cultural Identities

There might be any number of factors leading to a woman's identifying herself as a Goddess feminist, not least of which would be factors of sexual preference, religious and political conviction, temperament and

spiritual taste. Some might wish to be free from the apparently inter-
minable struggle to negotiate an (eco)feminist voice in the often hostile
environment of traditional religions. They might prefer to enjoy Goddess religion's unambiguous affirmation of the female character of the
divine and of the divinity of femaleness. Some might have a taste for the
earthiness and practicality of Goddess religion. Others might find its distinctive woman-centred rituals and magical practices (in feminist Wicca
especially) more directly numinous and empowering than Jewish or
Christian prayer and ritual (in which politically and spiritually affirming
rites of passage for women and girls *as* women are usually notably
absent).

Trying to unknot the tangled skein of personal, social and intellectual
motivations that knits together a Goddess feminist spiritual/political
identity is not always a rewarding task. Like any contemporary social or
religious phenomenon that is both nascent and in flux, Goddess feminism is, for the researcher, something of moving target. Not only can it
be difficult to gauge the numbers of Goddess feminists and the precise
place of Goddess feminism within the Goddess movement, it is also
difficult to generalize about or classify the women who align themselves
with Goddess feminism and their reasons for doing so. Goddess feminists
have a basic spiritual orientation and basic political convictions in common, but these can be expressed in quite different ways. This combi-
nation of diversity and commonality among Goddess feminists can be
illustrated by a comparison of personal perspective and style among six
Goddess feminists with whom I am acquainted. (These six women's
names have been changed to protect their privacy):

Miriam (British and in her late 50s) is a practising Jew on the alternative wing of the Reform Jewish community. She is a Jungian psychotherapist and scholar working to retrieve the suppressed goddess traditions of esoteric and ancient Judaism. All but the most alternative of
Jews would question her Jewishness and would probably regard her as
Pagan, though she would not see herself so.

Sarah (American and in her early 40s) is also a Jewish, feminist, Jungian psychotherapist who, like Miriam, uses goddess archetypes thera-
peutically with her clients. Lilith (the rebellious, exiled 'first wife' of
Adam who is demonized in traditional Judaism but who is honoured by
Jewish feminists as the 'first' of their number) is of particular spiritual
and political importance to her. Some years ago Sarah hired a hall in the
American equivalent of a British Reform synagogue to celebrate her

daughter's menarche and then, after the rabbi had stated his disapproval in no uncertain terms, 'left' Judaism. Both she and Miriam dress conventionally, adopting no countercultural badges of identity.

Anne (American and in her early 40s) is, again, a Jungian psychotherapist and counsellor. She uses the Goddess for healing and political purposes but also uses loosely Christian feminist resources in rituals and would resist an exclusively Pagan or Christian label. Although of European ancestry, she wears the clothes and heavy silver and turquoise jewellery that are strongly reminiscent of traditional Native Americans and which suggest her New Age or post-biblical inclinations.

Sophie (American and in her late 40s) is an academic from a secular feminist background. She became actively involved in Goddess feminist ritual and political protest or direct action through her research into feminist witchcraft. Her image fuses countercultural elements and the wearing of Goddess symbols as jewellery with a more conventionally professional style.

Mary (British and in her mid 30s) is a self-identified post-Christian lesbian Goddess feminist who dresses in a countercultural style and wears a small silver replica of a labrys[8] that immediately conveys her spiritual feminist sympathies to other like-minded women. She is active in the ecofeminist movement.

Penny (British and in her late 40s) is a self-identified Pagan whose first experience of witchcraft was gained in a feminist, women-only Dianic coven. Her feminist principles have informed the organization and practice of the present non-Dianic coven in which she is a priestess. She also has a strong theoretical interest in thealogy. Penny lives and dresses in a clearly countercultural style.

While these are merely random, anecdotal, illustrative examples and do not in any way constitute statistical evidence, my sample is nonetheless, indicative of several notable sociological features of the feminist

---

8. The labrys is a double-bladed axe, images of which have been found in Crete, whose ancient Minoan culture is often cited as an important example of a matristic or matrifocal society, and at Delphi, the oldest Greek shrine to the Goddess. The labrys, often worn by spiritual feminists as a pendant, now symbolizes the empowering 'memory' of matristic societies. It is a metaphor for a spiritual feminist critical engagement with patriarchy that owes much to the work of Mary Daly. Daly understands the labrys as a symbol of radical feminist philosophy's ability to cut cleanly through patriarchal language, theology and philosophy with wit, wisdom and judgment. (See, e.g., Daly 1984: ix; 1993: 151).

wing of the Goddess movement. To begin with, the sample clearly reflects how, at present at least, women under thirty seem less likely to be attracted to spiritual feminism than those in their thirties and beyond. One reason for this might be that women who have come to maturity between the late 1960s and the mid 1980s, when the British and American women's movement was confident, active and generally more radical than it is today, are more likely to make a connection between the power and energy generated by the revival of the Goddess with that generated by the women's movement.

All but one of the Goddess women in this sample are from an educated, middle-class background, reflecting Goddess feminism's predominantly educated, middle-class constituency, as well as that of feminism itself (See Eller 1993: 12-37). Half of the women in my sample have a psychotherapeutic interest in Goddess religion and spirituality, again reflecting the strong professional and theoretical link between thealogy and psychotherapy. However, while those who speak at and attend conferences and workshops tend to be waged it would be wrong to assume that all Goddess feminists are prosperous and have a middle-class economic status. (Barbara Mor cowrote the highly influential *Great Cosmic Mother* while she was on welfare and later awaited its production and the royalties it would earn while a bag lady on the streets of Tucson, Arizona [Sjöö and Mor 1991: xiv-xv].)

Both of the Jewish women in the sample still have lesser or greater emotional and cultural attachments to Jewishness (as distinguished from the orthodox observance of Jewish law), and one maintains regular connections with the alternative Jewish community. In my perception at least, this is common among Jewish women who celebrate the Goddess and/or the goddesses of Jewish tradition. (Even as I write, Starhawk—a Jewish Pagan and perhaps the best-known of all Goddess feminists—is planning to hold a Goddess/earth-centred Passover meal or *Seder* at Glastonbury, a notable centre of British Goddess religion.) For reasons I discuss in Chapter 1 of this study, Jewish Goddess women seem to retain stronger connections with their tradition than do Goddess women of Christian background with their tradition.

Some research shows Jews to be statistically over-represented in Goddess feminism and Neo-Paganism as a whole, but these findings are highly debatable.[9] More generally though, all the women in my sample

9.   In 1980 Gordon Melton gave a paper to the Society for the Scientific Study of Religion showing Jews to be doubly represented in American Neo-Paganism.

are white and the perceived lack of an ethnic mix in Goddess feminism is something of a vexed issue. American spiritual feminism does have some well-known non-white figures in its numbers such as the Native American Paula Gunn Allen (Laguna Pueblo/Sioux) and Dhyani Ywahoo (Cherokee), Ava Su Gan Wei (Chinese–American) and the Santería priestess and witch Luisah Teish. Nonetheless, Goddess feminism is still overwhelmingly Caucasian, and regularly expresses concern at being so (Eller 1993: 18-20).

Not surprisingly, spiritual feminism has a far larger proportion of lesbians than have other religious traditions (Adler 1986: 184). Although, in the United States at least, the political influence of Dianic Wicca[10] seems to be waning and its lesbian separatist element diminishing,[11] lesbians are still attracted to Goddess feminism in that it is surely the most thoroughly woman-identified of any contemporary religion on earth. The majority of spiritual feminists are not, however, lesbians, even if lesbians are statistically over-represented (Adler 1986: 184; Eller 1993: 20-21). By way of a comparison, all but one of the women in my sample would define themselves as heterosexual and are or have been married. None, to my knowledge, has suffered sexual abuse as child or adult. However, women who have suffered childhood sexual abuse or rape, battering or psychological abuse at the hands of men are often attracted to Goddess feminism as its separatist elements particularly tend to ignore (or even vilify) men and the roles and symbology of masculinity in religion. All Goddess feminism, by its very nature, is a profoundly effective means of restoring women's damaged confidence and self-esteem.

It may be that an 'identikit' picture of a Goddess feminist can no more be produced than could be for a practitioner of any of the world's

Margot Adler's own research broadly confirms this (Adler 1986: 444). However, Eller regards the view that Jews (and Catholics) are disproportionately represented among spiritual feminists as 'a popular conception' that she would hesitate to support (1993: 22-23). Nonetheless, she notes some anecdotal evidence that confirms Jewish over-representation.

10. Dianic Wicca was originally a women-only form of lesbian feminist witchcraft. Today, it is less likely to be separatist, but remains the most woman and Goddess-centred form of contemporary witchcraft.

11. W. Griffin, 'Diana's Daughters: Postmodern Priestessing in America', paper given at the conference '"Ambivalent Goddesses": An Exploration of the Current State of the Study of Goddesses and Goddess Spirituality', at King Alfred's College of Higher Education, Winchester, 26 March 1997.

religions. But Goddess feminism has cultural characteristics that make this task yet more difficult. For while Goddess feminism exemplifies a modern drive for the emancipation of the oppressed, it is also a product of the late modern (or some might say 'postmodern') turn in non-orthodox, religious observance over the last twenty years or so. Arguably, late modern or postmodern culture has produced distinctly eclectic, post-traditional religious identities that are globalist in outlook and defy neat classification. By this I mean that in late modernity global capitalism, global communication systems and mass travel have together rendered all religious and cultural identities more complex and shifting than they appear to have been, say, two hundred years ago. Consumerist attitudes to religion have allowed people to select and reconstitute elements of various traditions to suit the spiritual and aesthetic requirements of their open, usually leaderless, plural religious identity. Contemporary seekers can be introduced to a plurality of spiritualities and practices, making it difficult (and perhaps unnecessary) to define their religious allegiance in anything other than compound classifications. Goddess feminism typifies this trend. For whilst Goddess feminism has a highly distinctive spiritual mood and, in the Goddess, a distinct object of celebration, its political and ecological spirit is common to most European and American religious feminists and indeed all those on the holistic left.

Goddess religion is also situated on the boundaries of older Pagan and biblical religions and the gradual dissolution or reconfiguration of old world views. The world's religions are never static, monolithic entities, but spiritual feminism is intentionally a fluid and permeable category of religious belief and practice. It seems clear that any boundary defining the Goddess movement in distinction from other progressive movements—including feminist ones—is and should be a permeable one. Such divisions as exist between Goddess feminists and other alternative political and spiritual groupings are not, at root, institutionally or externally fixed; identities are created (and uncreated) in the process of an individual situating her or himself within one or more overlapping communities.

Naomi Goldenberg, one of first women to identify and undertake the thealogical project, rightly associates the notion of a single, fixed religious identity with the masculinist creation of territories defended by potentially violent tribal loyalties to a single divine or human power and authority. Feminism is, for her and other spiritual feminists, about the

need to feel the 'empathy, involvement, and identity beyond our particular tribe' that is essential to the renunciation of control and dominance
and the cause of global peace. Feminism can 'transform the human community by questioning the established social groupings and by encour-
aging us all to realise how much we are implicated in the fate of one
another.' Tribalism is threatened by those who enjoy multiple, connected identities; by 'the female sense of diversity within self-hood' For
this reason, Goldenberg argues that 'the world is in need of people who
can feel several loyalties, several affinities, several identities' (1990: 64-
67)—as so many Goddess feminists do.

Bearing Goldenberg's remarks in mind, it seems both fruitless and
divisive to try to establish a single Goddess feminist perspective entirely
separate from and in competition with other religious and political perspectives. It may be that the study of Goddess feminism can be best
approached less by sociological methodologies than by empathetic historical and philosophical discussion of its religious and political convictions. Goddess feminism came into being by differentiating itself from
the secular women's movement; thealogy came into being by distinguishing itself from feminist theology's attempt to reconfigure the God
of Western theism in the light of women's experience and feminist
theory. Two types of religious feminism emerged out of differences
over the style and content of feminist politics and out of different
answers to the question of allegiance to the biblical traditions. It is to
these issues of thealogy's continuities and discontinuities with other sorts
of religious feminism that we now turn.

Chapter One

The Boundaries of Thealogy

I propose that we face the possibility of a contradiction inherent in the idea "feminist Christian theologian." I suggest that the idea "feminist theologian" implies an evolutionary leap in consciousness beyond "Christian" and that the word "feminist" does something to the meaning content of the word "theologian." . . . After stepping outside the circle of Christian theology we find ourselves in unexplored territory (Daly 1972).[1]

From Theology to Thealogy

Although there is evidence of women's criticism of and protest against religious inequality from about 1500, religious feminism as we know it dates from the mid nineteenth century. But little from nineteenth-century religious feminism can be said to have produced Goddess religion itself. Most First Wave Christian feminists wanted opportunities to exercise their feminine expertise in the public as well as private sphere (indeed, in effect, they refused to acknowledge any such distinction). Theirs (and evangelical feminists' particularly) was a self-sacrificial, maternalist spirituality founded on the Christian morality of service in Christ's name. Certainly, Goddess feminism has interesting continuities with nineteenth century evangelical feminism's sense of the distinctive spirituality and moral worth of femininity. (Banks 1986: 243, 249) But while contemporary spiritual feminists have developed nineteenth-century Christian feminists' sense of the special moral and spiritual value of womanhood, nineteenth-century evangelical ideologies of domestic and self-sacrificial feminine sanctity are too conservative to be palatable to nearly all contemporary religious feminists. Spiritual feminists are more

---

1. Quoted by Daly (1993: 174).

likely to regard the nineteenth-century theosophists such as Annie
Besant and Francis Swiney as their foremothers (Jeffreys 1985: 27-53;
Burfield 1983: 27-56). So too, a direct line can be traced from Elizabeth
Cady Stanton and Matilda Joslyn Gage's radical call for women to reject
ecclesiastical and scriptural authority to the iconoclastic spirit of contem-
porary Goddess feminism (Weaver 1989: 49).

Generally speaking, though, First Wave 'strong-minded' women (as
they were often known) established patterns of protest, activism and
scriptural interpretation in the nineteenth century which paved the way
for the Second Wave of religious feminism. This latter began in the late
1960s and early 70s and produced feminist theology and, close on its
heels, thealogy. Second Wave feminism did not discover the link between male-dominated religion and the disempowerment of women by
itself. That had already become apparent to a number of (proto) feminists in the nineteenth-century. By the very early 1970s statements like
Kate Millet's, 'Patriarchy has God on its side' (1972: 51) prompted all
feminists to question the relation of the masculinity of God and sexual-
political oppression. In the intellectually permissive, egalitarian and sec-
ularist mood of the time it was inevitable that feminists would begin to
make more extensive connections between the absence of female images
of the divine and female social marginality than their nineteenth-century
foremothers had done. Secular feminists were predisposed to reject all
religion as intrinsically oppressive and thereafter ignore it, but feminists
with religious inclinations wanted to pursue alternative theologies and,
as in the case of Goddess feminists, an alternative religion.

Although, as I have already indicated, the boundary between feminist
theology and thealogy is a permeable one and a significant number of
Jewish and Christian Goddess-honouring women feel neither 'in' nor
'out' of their traditions (Dinkelspiel 1981; Litwoman 1981; Raphael
1998a), the feminist movement is marked by a history of alignment with
either radical or reformist feminist political theory, of which the division
between radical/pagan and reformist/biblical feminism is a product and
a microcosm. Feminist theory can be very broadly categorized as either
liberal/reformist or radical/romantic (Tong 1992). Feminism's earliest
form was that of a liberal Enlightenment call for the rights and dignity of
'man' to be extended to women as well. When the Second Wave of
feminism emerged in the mid-1960s it rejected domestic, maternal, feminine roles for women as stereotypical and reflecting and perpetuating
sexual inequality. Early Second Wave feminism was primarily concerned

that women should have equality of career opportunities with men. Reformist feminism wanted to minimize the difference between women and men. In this period and beyond, essentialist accounts of femaleness as 'naturally' or physiologically intuitive or caring, were rejected by reformists who believed that female difference was of cultural rather than natural origin (Ruether 1983: 111).

But from the late 1960s onwards, there was, in some quarters, a growing sense that women *as* women had a distinctively pacific contribution to make to the well-being of the earth and its human and natural inhabitants. 'Radical' feminism—as it was to be styled—moved outside the male-dominated civil rights and New Left movements of students and intellectuals of which it had been a part. These supposedly egalitarian movements came to be perceived as hostile or indifferent to feminism. Radical feminists rejected these projects as patriarchal and had no desire for equality on what remained patriarchal terms. As can be seen quite clearly in thealogy, radical feminism does not see patriarchy merely as the abuse of male economic and religious and familial power, or as an unequal division of power, but as the very nature of power in male-dominated societies. Radical feminism, or 'cultural' feminism (as it is sometimes known), advocates instead a politically (and often physically) separatist way of life focused on the celebration of female difference and traditionally female activities and relationships in a post-patriarchal context. Cultural feminism (of which Goddess feminism's emphasis on spiritual and biological difference is a particular religious form) is, in this respect, almost the reverse of reformist feminism.

It is not difficult to see how this basic split between radical and reform movements in Second Wave feminism correlates with and produces a division between religious feminist writers and academics; the reformists formulating a new inclusive, relational paradigm within the biblical tradition, and the radicals formulating a gynocentric paradigm outside it. As a rule, the reformist project has sought to distance femaleness from biology. Reformist feminism argues that a gynocentric focus on female bodily experience, the femaleness of nature, and the sexuality and immanence of the Goddess is unhelpfully ahistorical, apolitical (because it removes women from the cultural spheres in which political change is achieved) and confirms patriarchal accounts of women as essentially natural and therefore sub-rational.

Goddess feminism believes, however, that it has, on its own political terms, done the reverse and celebrates the ecologically grounded naturalness of sexual energy and the wildness of natural—post- or meta-patriarchal—being (Raphael 1997: 55-72). Of course, it would be wrong to suggest that contemporary reformist religious feminism does not celebrate embodiment and the life-affirming quality of erotic connection. Conversely, it would be wrong to say that radical religious feminists are *only* interested in nature and sexual embodiment at the expense of female intellection. However, reformist religious feminism does not make female biology the central generative locus of subversive religious meaning, as spiritual feminism has done (Raphael 1996b *passim*).

From the mid-1970s onwards both feminist biblical ('reformist') theologians and post-biblical ('radical') thealogians were to mount a significant emancipatory critique of patriarchal religion and theology—especially that of the Western Abrahamic traditions.[2] First of all, feminist theologians and scholars of religion undertook the massive task of pointing out the misogynistic and androcentric nature of texts, laws, rituals and hierarchies in patriarchal religions. This was, and remains, a task of demonstrating how religious language, texts, laws, rituals and other practices (as well as the patriarchal scholarship that documents them) deny the full humanity of women as subjects of their own religious experience. Patriarchal religion profoundly damaged women's self-esteem and, therefore spiritually and politically disempowers them. The all-pervasiveness of religious sexism has desensitized believers to its offensiveness to women and its harm to the ethical standing of the given religion. The feminist critique was therefore a task of consciousness-raising, enabling people to 'read' a patriarchal religion as the ground and index to a society's ultimate values, as well as the central medium of its ideology.

The task of demonstrating how religion has been distorted (or constituted) by sexism is a vital preliminary. But that task must be complemented by a more positive one: that of recovery, reclamation and reconstruction of the liberative ground and elements of religion. Reformist feminism has noted the ambiguity of traditional meanings and intentions and the existence of prophetic counter-traditions within the dominant traditions. Both radical and reformist religious feminists have been engaged in the development of new, non-hierarchical theo/alogies which

---

2.   The phrase 'Abrahamic religion' indicates a group of originally Middle Eastern religions (namely, Judaism, Christianity and Islam) stemming from the narrative of God's promise to bless Abraham and his descendants in Genesis.

demand the elite male's relinquishment of his religious, political and discursive privileges. Feminist theo/alogies are using female and non gender-specific imagery to evolve new models of God that comprehensively transform what it is we mean by God (McFague 1983). Jewish and Christian feminist transformations of the patriarchal God have involved a critical editing of traditional theology, and have reclaimed and incorporated female symbols and biblical divinities that describe aspects of the femaleness of that God. Feminist theologians not only image God as Mother; the ancient titles of Hochmah/Sophia are also used to denote her wisdom and Shekhinah to denote her immanence on earth. For thealogy, which does not regard the Bible as a sacred or even useful text, new models of the divine are constituted by femaleness. Nonetheless, *all* feminist models of the divine are, by their feminist nature, politically alternative and promote egalitarian social and ecological relationships.

Despite sharing with feminist theology close ties of origin, political values and experience of the injustices of patriarchal religion, thealogy also has historical roots of its own that carried its development on a slightly different trajectory than that of feminist theology. I alluded to these roots in the introduction to this study, but can elaborate upon my discussion here.

There are a number of specific historical moments from which one can date the origins of thealogy and the different direction it would take to that of other religious feminisms. First, thealogy's departure from the biblical traditions can be traced to the Enlightenment's criticism of what it perceived to be the intellectual and political tyranny of the Church (see Eilberg-Schwartz 1989: 77-95). Many Enlightenment philosophers were instead attracted to the classical learning of Pagan antiquity and to Paganism as a religion of nature (that is, a religion of human reason, rather than faith in what seemed to them to be ecclesiastical superstition) (Eilberg-Schwartz 1989: 80-81).

Secondly, thealogy's religious aesthetic—its sense of the numinosity of the natural—can be traced to early nineteenth-century romanticism's attraction to the instinctual and the untamed, to religious exotica, reconstructed Pagan traditions, and its antipathy to industrialization as aesthetically and spiritually disharmonious with nature.

Thirdly, the radical, alternative nature of thealogical politics can be understood as a product of the neo-romantic hippie counterculture of the 1960s and 70s. The hippie movement attracted many critical thinkers who were involved in the peace movement and were in search of ecstatic visionary and erotic experience, non-materialistic communitarian life-styles, sexual freedom and equality, alternative medicine and non-biblical spiritualities. Within the liberal academy of this period too, religious scholarship was looking towards a post-traditional, secular society as a way of demystifying and liberating the sacred from traditional ecclesial authority (see Culpepper 1991; Scott 1971). As Pam Lunn notes, the civil rights movement, protest against the Vietnam war, and the beginnings of the post-colonial era were all factors in Goddess feminism's spiritual/political development. Goddess religion could also be said to share in the search for spiritual and political authenticity or 'roots' of many in the Jewish and Black communities of the time (1993: 33).

In a wider context, sociologists of religion have noted how Europe and America have not undergone the wholesale secularization they had predicted in the 1960s. Although some forms of traditional religion have declined, there has been a bipolar growth in new religious groupings. At one pole there has been the growth of fundamentalism among large sectors of the Jewish, Christian, Hindu and Islamic communities and in the authoritarian, well-financed, new religious movements such as the Reverend Sun Myung Moon's Unification Church. Religions at this pole are generally right-wing, conservative and patriarchal in character. At the other pole, there has been a rapid growth in Europe and America of broadly left-wing, post-traditional, post-institutional, individualistic, immanentist[3] forms of religion and spirituality, of which Goddess feminism is a part.

More specifically, the Wiccan revival of the 1950s, subsequent to the British repeal of acts forbidding witchcraft, enabled Wiccans to practice their religion openly. Wicca is a European earth religion honouring both female and male divinity (giving pre-eminence to the female divine principle) and offering the magical empowerment of *all* who participate. It was, and is, therefore, attractive to many feminists who, despite their vehement rejection of patriarchal religion, were still in search of an ecologically and politically nourishing spirituality. In particular, feminist versions of Wicca flourished in the green, alternative, activist circles of the 1970s and 80s in Britain and America.

---

3. 'Immanentist' religion emphasizes divine presence in the world and downplays the transcendence of divinity as 'above' or wholly other to the world.

Some date the beginnings of spiritual feminism to the radical feminist consciousness-raising groups of the early 1970s. These have been seen as 'the natural predecessor' of contemporary spiritual feminist groups and ritual practice (Eller 1993: 43-44; Adler 1986: 182). In CR groups (as they were known) women would form a circle and give each other much-needed space and time to express feelings and share experiences and ideas. As the experiences articulated were recognized to be common to many or most of the women involved, this reinforced the sense that 'the personal is political'—that CR was a political as well as therapeutic process. The first issue of the journal *WomanSpirit* in the spring of 1974 was to consolidate the work of consciousness-raising groups (Christ 1983: 246; Adler 1986: 182-83).

Even though the contemporary Goddess movement came into being in the first half of the 1970s, there is no doubt that from 1976 onwards, the pace of its development increased significantly. That development might have been accelerated by the hostility to thealogy that began to be apparent even among liberals within the religious community. As Carol Christ remembers, after the religious feminist community had found its feet, most of her friends and academic colleagues began to express 'serious reservations' about Goddess religion: 'Male theologians sympathetic to feminism drew the line at the Goddess. I felt profoundly isolated. While I had expected criticism from male colleagues, I had not experienced it from other feminists . . . I stopped writing' (1987: 204). Between 1976 and 1979 it became possible to see what was to be known as 'thealogy' beginning to distinguish itself from feminist theology. In April 1976 over a thousand women gathered for a three-day women's spirituality conference called 'Through the Looking Glass: A Gynergenetic Experience', during which 'many women said they felt, for the first time, that a new "women's culture" was a reality' (Adler 1986: 225). 1979 was a key year. On 31 October 1979 (Samhain or All Hallow's Eve—Paganism's most numinous day of the year), Starhawk's groundbreaking *The Spiral Dance* was published in San Francisco and Margot Adler's *Drawing Down the Moon* was published in New York:

> Under the light of a not quite full October moon, therefore, from coast to coast, American feminists were invited to consider a viable religious alternative, a new religion claiming to be a revival of 'the Old Religion' dating back to the beginning of time (Weaver 1989: 51).

1979 also saw the publication of Mary Daly's *Gyn/Ecology*, Naomi Goldenberg's *Changing of the Gods* and Carol Christ and Judith Plaskow's

collection of essays, *Womanspirit Rising*. Whilst *Womanspirit Rising* included essays by Christian and Jewish reformist feminist theologians, it
culminated in Christ's persuasive article presenting women with reasons
for adopting a Goddess spirituality (1992: 273-86). By then a woman's
choice of whether or not to stay with the tradition of her birth had
become a significant one. By 1989, the publication date of their next
collaborative undertaking, Judith Plaskow and Carol Christ had gone
their separate religious ways; one to the reconstruction of Jewish theology and tradition, and the other to Goddess religion (1989: v).

Negotiating the Boundaries between
Feminist Theology and Thealogy

Feminist theology does not, by its nature, articulate a new religion, but
proposes a Judaism, Christianity or Islam transformed by the full and
equal inclusion of women in all dimensions of the religion. This can
involve the reformation of the religion by a restoration of the original
egalitarianism believed to have been instituted by its founder(s). Thealogy, however, conceives itself as having made a radical break from
Western monotheism such as was symbolized by Mary Daly's dramatic
exit or exodus from the Harvard Divinity School Chapel in 1971. Having been invited to be the first woman to preach there, her sermon was
a courageous prophetic challenge to the religion and politics of her
hosts: a religion that, she claimed in her sermon, has 'drained and co-
opted' women's energies, and denies women's humanity. She refused
the role of 'token' woman preacher and concluded (ironically, in good
biblical style): 'we must go away'; 'go out from the land of our fathers
into an unknown place' (Clark and Richardson 1977: 265-71). Or
again, Monica Sjöö and others declared 'the end of patriarchy' and
patriarchal religion by dancing and drumming before the altar in Bristol
Cathedral during a Sunday morning service in 1993 (1993: 22-23).

Oversimplifying somewhat, the history of feminist discourse could be
described as that of a series of negotiations and splits between radical and
reformist feminist theorists. Although the boundary between feminist
theology and thealogy can be a permeable one, the basic division between radical/Pagan and reformist/biblical feminism is a historical product and a microcosm of this internal dissension in the feminist community. As Mary Jo Weaver has chronicled, (1989: 54-56) wherever there
has been a challenge (even if implicit) for women to 'choose sides'

between radical and reformist religion this has sparked a good deal of political and academic controversy. Although some women have denied that any absolute distinction between radical and reformist feminist theo/ alogy exists and that each 'camp' has a spectrum of perspectives within it, there is, nonetheless, a real distinction between those feminists who choose to stay and transform their tradition and those who make a decision to leave it and who have no intention of observing its rituals and festivals again.[4]

Conflict between these two camps crystallized in a somewhat acrimonious debate between Rosemary Ruether and Carol Christ (and their respective supporters) from 1979 until about 1982, and its main points of contention are not yet, and perhaps cannot be, resolved. After the publication of Starhawk's *The Spiral Dance* in 1979, Ruether suggested that Goddess feminists were misreading both the Bible—which has a liberative potential—and the ancient historical goddesses which, as the constructs of patriarchal power, do not (Ruether 1979: 303-11). Carol Christ, who had left the Presbyterian church, responded to Ruether in the journal *WomanSpirit*, arguing that the biblical tradition's masculine language for God and the religious intolerance of the prophets could never form the basis of a truly feminist theology. Further public criticism of Ruether by Goldenberg, Christ and other 'radical' religious feminists resulted in Ruether's second article, 'Goddesses and Witches: Liberation and Countercultural Feminism' (1980: 842-47), and probably accounts for its waspish tone.[5] In this article she again criticized Goddess feminists for their escapism, separatism, misconceived historiography and simplistically dualistic anthropology that equated women with immanence and biophilia, and men with transcendence and necrophilia —issues and criticisms to which this study will return.

---

4. The process of separation from a mainstream tradition is rarely easy. As Dinkelspiel relates, 'We lose the security of a consistent religious system, the security of churches which serve as the plausibility structures for those systems, the security of unproblematic participation in liturgies and church practices and the security of unquestioning acceptance of known images, symbols and stories (1981: 3).

5. See for example, Ruether's summarizing view of Goddess feminism at that time (1980: 847): 'There is nothing objectionable in the effort to create a feminist spirituality as such. But actually to do so is both more difficult and more dangerous than one might realize, and demands both greater modesty and maturity than those still deeply wounded by patriarchal religion have generally been able to muster.'

Goddess religion is now classified as post-Christian (Woodhead 1993: 167-70). This term does not only mean that a person has left Christianity behind (in which case the word 'Christian' would be redundant), it means that post-Christian women and men are still in varying degrees of serious and sharply critical engagement with the Christian tradition to which they may have once belonged. Although thealogy may be described as post-Christian, that term is not the exclusive property of Goddess feminists. For example, Daphne Hampson is commonly classified as post-Christian but she is not a Goddess feminist; she has simply left the Church for feminist reasons (1990; 1996). Mary Daly is most often described as a post-Christian philosopher/thealogian (or as she would now write the term, 'Postchristian', as she does not do Christianity the honour of capitalization). For Daly, 'Postchristian' denotes that after leaving the Church she did not want to become a secular feminist; she still 'longed passionately for the transcendence that was held prisoner and choked by [patriarchal] religion and theology' (1993: 174).

However, Goddess feminists would not usually call themselves 'post-Christian' as the term is a largely academic classification. Goddess feminists often call themselves 'Goddess women'. And the term 'post-Jewish' or 'post-Judaic' is very rarely used by academics or Goddess feminists of Jewish birth. This is because being and feeling Jewish need not entail observance of Jewish law or faith in the Jewish God. For non-observant Jews, Jewishness consists in having been born of a Jewish mother into an often vibrant cultural and familial environment that has almost always been under severe pressure from racism and anti-Judaism, such that whatever a person comes to believe about God they remain Jewish. As we shall find to be the case of Jewish women who celebrate the Goddess, Jews almost always 'feel' Jewish and have residual loyalties to Jewish culture whatever their current state of belief.

By contrast, Mary Daly has definitely left the Church; it is for her, empty of value. There is a marked difference between her reformist first book, *The Church and the Second Sex* (1968) and her second, *Beyond God the Father* (1973). In this latter text Daly states a position with which she remains in substantial agreement, though she has elaborated it considerably since then. In *Beyond God the Father* she argues that patriarchy is legitimated by (Judaeo) Christianity—an inherently necrophilic world view that supplants and drains women's energies and establishes the pre-eminence of the masculine God and Jesus over all other beings. In that religious context women's liberation is, fundamentally, a liberation from the institutionalization of non–being and a call for women to confront patriarchy with the existential courage born of sisterhood and the energies of the emergent post–patriarchal self.

Thealogians do not merely despair of the rate or degree to which the biblical model of God might be reformed, but of the masculine, disembodied modes by which the father-god creates nature, and his believers traditionally relate to nature. Thealogians do not think it worthwhile to apply a feminist hermeneutic to the biblical text, feeling that its patriarchal nature is not detachable from its (only occasionally liberative) messages. Monotheistic religions founded within a patriarchal culture by a male founder and predicated upon the will of a male divinity can have no original meta-patriarchal essence. Goddess women deny the authority of the biblical texts (even as read by reformist feminists) and reject the 'masculine' linearity of the biblical temporal scheme. In terms of secular political rights, Goddess women support Christian and Jewish women's right to ordination. But they are also mystified by what they (perhaps unfairly) perceive to be biblical feminists' desire to mediate a divine father–son relationship to the exclusion of divine mother–daughter relationships.[6]

Yet despite the clear differences of opinion between feminist theologians and thealogians over the value of the biblical text, the history of the Church and the virtues of remaining within a predominantly patriarchal tradition, the difference between theology and thealogy *as spiritualities* may, as I have indicated, only be one of emphasis or degree. As Linda Woodhead has persuasively argued, not only is there considerable overlap between feminist theology and much contemporary Christian theology and spirituality that is not explicitly feminist, there is also considerable overlap with thealogical spirituality. Woodhead finds the distinction between post-Christian feminist spirituality (which is usually thealogical) and liberal forms of Christian feminist spirituality a false one. Woodhead writes,

> I believe that the only difference . . . is that reformist feminist theologians are happier than post-Christian ones to use the Jewish and Christian traditions as a fruitful source of symbols and stories, and sometimes they are prepared to remain within the church. Beyond this, their spiritualities seem to me identical and equally post-Christian (1993: 171).

6.   This ambivalence comes across in a letter by Monica Sjöö (1994: 15-16) where she gives an account of the vigil she and other Goddess feminists mounted

Comparing Ruether's work to that of post-Christians, and examining Ruether's emphasis on women's experience, her discarding most of Christian tradition bar the prophetic one, the use of non-Christian traditions in her work of the mid-1980s, her description of the divine as 'Primal Matrix', and her foundational ecofeminism, Woodhead concludes (perhaps overstating her case a little), 'I can find nothing substantive in her vision with which the post-Christian feminists should really want to disagree' (1993: 171). While an important reformist like Rosemary Ruether has strong reservations about thealogy's historiographical methods and assumptions and about its political effectiveness, she does not, it would appear, reject the search for the Goddess or for female symbols for the divine as such (Weaver 1989: 51-52). It is, as Pam Lunn points out, not always easy to distinguish the Goddess from female images of God in Christian and Jewish feminist writing and practice (1993: 19-20 n. 1). The foundational impetus of reformist and radical religious feminism is the same. Both aim to retrieve female authenticity and history; both believe that one can be both religious and a feminist and that, indeed, religion, within a feminist paradigm, is politically as well as spiritually liberative. Reformist and radical religious feminists share much of the same left-wing ecological, anti-militarist and nurturant emphases.

Although Christian feminism can be critical of Goddess feminism, it is rarely as sharply critical of the latter as is secular feminism. There is a sense in which thealogy departs more from biblical feminism than (non-evangelical) biblical feminism does from thealogy. Judith Plaskow, perhaps the best-known Jewish feminist, is not a Goddess feminist but does regard some Jewish feminists' use of Goddess imagery as a way of extending the range of metaphors available to Jewish theology and a way of incorporating femaleness and women's experience into a true, that is, properly inclusive, monotheism (1991: 150-52).

So the frontier between thealogy and feminist theology is not always closed, at least on the side of feminist theology. In academia, thealogy is usually classified under the general heading of feminist theology. Feminist theology conferences typically have lecture and workshop slots for thealogians or for Christian and Jewish women who want to explore the female divinities of their own traditions. In the Women-Church movement too, it is common to find the practice of rituals (such as the

outside Bristol Cathedral on the day that the first women priests in the Church of England were ordained there in April 1994.

croning ritual) more commonly associated with thealogical than with feminist theological positions (McPhillips 1994: 115).

Only the most entrenched on each side refuse any links with the other. After all, both thealogians and feminist theologians belong to the feminist spirituality movement (a term with wider connotations than 'spiritual feminism', which usually connotes a more anti-biblical tendency). Spiritual feminists coming from observant Jewish or Christian backgrounds may, in any case, find it difficult or even unnecessary to eradicate all the comfortingly familiar motifs and rituals of their former religions from their current spirituality. This is especially the case if that religion were the one she grew up with and whose suppressed or subordinated female divinities like Mary (Queen of Heaven and Mother of God), Hochmah (Wisdom) and Shekhinah (the presence or indwelling of God) can readily be incorporated as goddesses into their thealogy. In celebrating the goddesses of many traditions Goddess feminism is inherently pluralistic. Starhawk claims that as she grows older, both her Jewish and her Pagan identities grow stronger. Acknowledging that this may seem contradictory, she writes, 'I am comfortable being both a Jew and a Pagan, celebrating Chanukhah and the Winter Solstice' (1990: xi).

The case of Jewish Goddess feminists and Jewish women on the 'left wing' of the Jewish feminist movement for whom the Jewish goddesses are religiously and psychologically significant, is a useful illustration of the blurring that can take place at the edges of spiritual feminist identities (Raphael 1998). Alix Pirani, for example, was inspired by Raphael Patai's *The Hebrew Goddess* (1967) and has claimed 'the Goddess of the Hebrews' from heterodox Jewish mystical writings on Hochmah, Shekhinah, Lilith, the Shabbat, the Matronit, and, from the biblical texts, the Canaanite Goddess Asherah who was probably once worshipped by syncretistic Israelites as Yahweh's consort (Pirani 1991: xi-xii). This process of retrieval has, for Pirani, 'brought Judaism alive again' and enabled her to return to the Jewish community that she had left at the age of 21. Indeed, she writes, 'My efforts to return to the Jewish community, religion, synagogue, then became identified with Her return' (1991: 166-67).

Pirani is not a Pagan but both a Goddess feminist and a Jew. Pirani's edited collection of essays, *The Absent Mother: Restoring The Goddess to Judaism and Christianity* is a good example of how exploring and reclaiming the Goddess need not necessitate exile from one's 'mother' tradition, indeed the Goddess can be seen to *be* the 'mother' tradition. Also, because, for Jews, Judaism can be a primarily social or cultural identity, a Jewish feminist's shift from a biblical to Pagan perspective need not entail a radical shift in cultural identity. Lynn Gottlieb, for example, runs workshops which help women to 'explore the Way of the Shekhinah [by] drawing on Jewish mystical traditions rooted in the Goddess'.[7]

So too, Gloria Orenstein is, like Pirani, inspired by Judaism's goddess heritage and the possibility of its matristic heritage (1991: 217). Orenstein feels 'both guilty about (her) search for the Goddess, and simultaneously ecstatic about discovering that our most ancient matriarch may even have revered Her'. Nonetheless, Orenstein and other Jewish women in the Goddess movement who, like her, maintain their Jewish identity, inevitably wrestle with the question of whether their Goddess feminism is Jewish or whether it represents a Pagan departure. While non-Jewish feminists continually remind Orenstein of her Jewishness (because secular feminists tend to be anti-Zionist and anti-religious), neither orthodox nor most liberal Jews would accept that a woman can be a Jewish Goddess feminist (1991: 220; 223). Even women rabbis, Orenstein has found, reject the possibility of Jewish Goddess feminism as a grave heresy. One woman rabbi responded to Orenstein's claiming the Jewishness of Goddess feminism with the words, 'But Gloria . . . we have been over this many times. Your Goddess is simply not Jewish. We have to make distinctions somewhere . . . We can't accept everything as Jewish' (1991: 219). Jewish women who have (re)integrated the Goddess into their religion and spirituality are isolated within the wider Jewish community. Judaism does not reject Jews who are agnostic but remain loyal to the Jewish people and traditions, because it does not enquire into people's state of faith. But remaining loyal to the Jewish people and traditions while worshipping a different god or, worse, goddesses, is not tolerated by any but the most alternative and 'open' of Jewish communities.

Goddess Feminism and Contemporary Paganism

For those women who believe that biblical symbolism and salvific schemata are inherently masculinist and anti-natural—in short, beyond feminist redemption—Paganism can provide a positive alternative. Paganism

---

7.   As advertised in *Goddessing Regenerated* 5 (1996: 3).

is an umbrella term for a number of earth religions celebrating the seasonal cycle.[8]

Contemporary Pagan mythology is typically structured by the relationship of the Goddess and her consort/son, the Horned God. The Goddess gives birth to the Horned God in mid-winter (December) marries him at the beginning of Summer (May) and sacrifices him to herself in Autumn (October), ensuring the fertility of the coming year. The term 'Pagan' derives from the Latin *paganus*, meaning country-dweller. Western Paganism's claim to be the native, 'original' religion of the British Isles, Old (pre-Christian) Europe and the ancient Near East makes it non- or extra-biblical and, in the view of Jews and Christians, suspect for that reason alone. However, the rural connotations of 'Pagan' remain important to contemporary Pagans who believe that rural people held onto their native religious identities for longer than the city dwellers or the elites who were earlier and more thoroughly converted to Israelite and Christian monotheism.

When feminists become disaffected with biblical religion, or have not previously adhered to any religion, they are most likely to turn to Paganism. This is a group of religions and spiritualities which—whatever their actual sexual-political shortcomings—at least honour a female principle, have feminist forms and usually adopt (or have forced upon them) a countercultural social and political posture.

What makes Paganism attractive to many post-Christian feminists is its offer of sexually inclusive, ecological teaching and practice. For most Pagans there must be a spiritual equilibrium and equality between the male and the female if the given rituals are to produce the cosmic, social and natural harmony they intend. Paganism is without a doctrine of inherent human sinfulness and, therefore, without correlating doctrines of redemption through law, sacrifice or a male saviour or messiah. Consequently, Pagan women are both free of any dependence on a male

8.   I have capitalized the term 'Pagan' for the same reasons as Margot Adler does (1986: 3-4), namely, that Pagans are practising a religion and deserve the same respect as do Jews and Christians who are generally not referred to in the lower case. Contemporary Paganism is often referred to as 'neo-Paganism', the prefix being usefully explained by Isaac Bonewits as referring to nature religions that are 'based upon older or Paleopagan religions; concentrating upon an attempt to retain the humanistic, ecological and creative aspects of these old belief systems while discarding their occasional brutal or repressive developments which are inappropriate' (Quoted in Adler 1986: 10).

salvific dispensation and no longer bear any of the moral responsibility for what is wrong with human existence—as Christian women especially have done in theologies premised on the sin and guilt of Eve.

While not all Goddess women are Pagan, all Goddess feminism draws to some extent from the Pagan traditions in that it is earth/ecology-based, celebrates female divinity under many names and is usually animistic to some degree.[9] Most Goddess feminists also celebrate the Pagan seasonal festivals and, like all Pagans, understand all aspects of culture, politics, art, the erotic, agriculture and so forth, as equally sacred. As is true of all Pagans, Goddess feminists do not proselytize. Women do not convert to Goddess religion in the conventional sense of the term, but, rather, get involved in it through reading, friendships with spiritual feminists, higher and continuing education, advertisements for local groups in spiritual feminist journals, and through other forms of alternative religion. Goddess women most often describe their changed religious identity as the result of a gradual shift in perception, often feeling that they have 'come home' or are 'remembering' perceptions of the Goddess that were previously unconscious, from a past life, or which were vivid childhood experiences gradually repressed by socialization into patriarchal 'reality' (Adler 1986: 15-20). For others, 'Pagan' is a merely convenient and not wholly inaccurate way for *others* to classify their spirituality. Mary Daly, speaking of herself and other post-Christians, has remarked, 'I doubt that any of us object to being called "pagan"' (1996: 181). In other words, 'Pagan' is an acceptable label for many feminist post-Christians, but is not always particularly important as a badge of identity.

British Goddess feminism (particularly feminist Wicca) is accepted by the wider contemporary Pagan community as one of a number of Pagan traditions. But Goddess feminists often have mixed feelings about 'mainstream' Paganism. It is commonly argued that masculine Pagan divinities like Odin, Thor and the Horned God give men as much license to exploit women as the biblical God. Indeed, it may be that the names and symbols for masculine divinity such as the Green Man, Oak Lad and

---

9.   Animistic religion does not distinguish between animate and inanimate objects, but sees all things in nature as conscious and partaking of the same vital energies. This perception of the world has been more characteristic of native religion, but the rise of ecological consciousness has done much to make animistic world views more widespread in Europe and America.

Horned God actually encourage an archaic, predatory macho sexuality.[10]

While Graham Harvey notes that most contemporary Pagans have been at least influenced by feminism (1997: 70), Cheryl Straffon (1994: 26-27) and other spiritual feminists are more doubtful of Pagan sexual politics. Although Paganism has aspects that are conducive to female empowerment, it can also demonstrate a sexism comparable to that of other mainstream religions. From a feminist perspective, Paganism is, like others of the world's religions, ambiguous; it gives women mixed messages.

Feminists routinely criticize the artistic representation of the Goddess in many forms of contemporary Paganism. Not surprisingly, Goddess feminists object to Paganism's common use of sexist, over-glamourized pictures of female divinity as exclusively white (too often, Nordic), nubile and naked. This 'air-brushed' (Maiden) goddess of male erotic imagining bears little relation to the fleshy goddess figurines of the Neolithic period, ignores the fierce, threatening and 'ugly' Crone aspect of the Goddess and alienates the Goddess from the 'ordinary' women who embody her. Such semi-pornographic images of the Goddess are not only spiritually and politically damaging, they also give Christian and Jewish critics further cause to doubt the religious and moral credibility of Paganism (Marsden-McGlynn 1993: 3-5).

For feminists, even more problematic than the representation of the Goddess, is Paganism's principle of sexual complementarity between men and women and the Goddess and the God. Generally speaking, this principle characterizes all conservative religion and claims that each sex has natural or divinely ordained roles that must be adhered to for the sake of social and spiritual harmony. These roles, in which the feminine complements the masculine, are roles articulated and controlled by men. Although many religious women clearly endorse these religious and social divisions of labour, their roles are usually played out in the private sphere and are subordinate and supplementary to those of men.

This kind of gender dualism is as inherent in mainstream (non-feminist) Paganism as it is in other patriarchal religions, and it is common among Pagans for women to be valued for intuition, domesticity, motherliness and beauty as the complement of masculine strength and rationality. Mainstream Pagans tend to regard the divine Lord and Lady—the

10. This is argued in a brief letter by Jackie (no surname given) from Bristol to the editors of *From the Flames* 13 (1994): 14.

masculine and feminine—as two complementary poles, where the former represents active and the latter passive roles, which must then be
balanced in each individual and in each ritual. Non-feminist Wiccans in
particular can be very hostile to feminist separatist Wiccans not only for
the way they disregard traditions of keeping rituals and spells secret to
the coven, but also because all-female separatist rituals and pantheons
lack the sexual balance required for them to be effective.

During the mid 1980s relations between American feminist and non-
feminist Pagans improved, and feminist Wiccan separatism began to
decline in favour of mixed feminist covens such as those established by
Starhawk (Adler 1986: 228). Nonetheless, for any Pagan feminist, especially separatist Wiccans, this traditional Pagan principle of sexual complementarity does, of course, represent a deeply retrograde anthropology. For Dianic Wiccans (who are often lesbian separatists) the power of
the female sacred does not require 'activation' by the male. The God-
dess/female self incorporates all modes of being—some of which might
be those of thinker or warrior, whose qualities are not monopolized by
men. To assign passive, 'feminine' characteristics to women in order to
create balance within rituals and partnerships is to domesticate and pacify
women and annuls all that feminism has achieved over the last thirty
years. By contrast, Dianic Wicca honours the Goddess as a self-sufficient
creative and transformatory power, whose activity does not require the
complement of male divinity. (Spiritual feminists often cite the prepon-
derance at given archaeological sites of single Neolithic figurines depicting priestesses or goddesses as evidence for the original independence of
the female from any male principle.) The Dianic Wheel of the Year is
driven by a purely female generativity. Here the Goddess does not give
birth to, marry or sacrifice the God; she is parthenogenetic (Raphael
1998). As Virgin and Mother, the Goddess gives birth to herself and all
life from the earth, her own body, in Spring and Summer. And as
Crone, the Goddess returns into the earth in the Autumn and Winter to
be reborn as Virgin (or Maiden) in the Spring.

Thealogy, Modernity and Postmodernism

To understand the origins and the future of thealogy it needs to be located not only in its religious context, but also in the widest histori-
cal/intellectual stream. A number of scholars of religion have recently
been preoccupied with the extent to which contemporary religion is

participant in the current 'postmodern' philosophical, literary and aesthetic shift away from the modern worldview. This is a highly complex assessment and not one that can be discussed in detail here. Nonetheless, no discussion of thealogy's place in, on and outside the boundaries of contemporary religious and intellectual movements would be complete without some examination of its participation in the intellectual shift that is called 'postmodernism'.

To understand the classification 'postmodern' it is first necessary to summarize its basic agreed features. The definition and content of the term 'postmodern' is a matter of controversy. Generally speaking, postmodernism represents a number of cultural and philosophical trends that criticize modernity. (Modernity is variously dated from the sixteenth-century Protestant Reformation or the eighteenth-century Enlightenment. Depending on whether one believes that Western culture *is* in a postmodern period, modernity runs up to the late 1960s or continues to describe the present)

Postmodern philosophy problematizes modern systems of thought and explanation with their pretensions to universal or total truth. Instead, postmodern thought emphasizes the contingency, contextuality or situatedness of all discourse, a consequence of which is that knowledge loses its foundation in controlling, transcendent divine or human (male) authorities. Knowledge is set loose from the traditional, elite anchor points of the Church and the academy. These authoritative institutions have foreclosed the boundaries of knowledge and experience in at least two ways. First, they have done so by 'totalizing' reality so as to lay claim to universal truth. And yet their reality is actually constructed and limited by the interests and extent of their own worldview. Secondly, the Church and the academy have controlled knowledge by limiting society's knowers to a privileged band of elite white males. This postmodern critique of institutional 'truth' has profound political implications. If, as the phrase goes, 'knowledge is power', then to relativize truth and examine whose interests truth serves, as postmodernism has done, is to undertake a massive displacement of power from the centre. The distinction between high and popular culture disappears as the hierarchies of knowledge dissolve. Knowledge can be chosen from a plurality of sources, because the notion of one certain truth has been shown to be a political construct; an illusion sustained by an elite that reflects and maintains its own structures of control.

Feminism has come to value postmodern ideas not least because modernity has failed, historically, to produce the liberation its Enlightenment rhetoric might have promised. Despite improvements in the status of (middle-class) women and the abolition of slavery and apartheid in most parts of the world, the modern patriarchal status quo remains much the same. As a methodological style postmodernism has also proved a useful way of challenging the androcentrism and dualism that has structured human relations by such gendered divisions as nature/ culture, rational/irrational, body/spirit—leaving 'woman' as the negative reference point against which men define their own values and their value as men (Jay 1991: 89-106).

However, many feminists are also wary of postmodern thinking. After all, if nothing is absolutely right and true then feminism's search for global justice is undermined, as is the recurrent religious feminist truth-claim that women's ways of relating to others are morally preferable to those of patriarchal men. Postmodernism may help to shift the male elite's hold on the generation of knowledge, but it probably has little to offer towards the religio-political resolution of conflict and inequality (See Hekman 1990; Nicholson 1990).

Where, then, might thealogy be said to be positioned within the modern/postmodern continuum? For all its criticism of modernity, and the scientism and colonialism that modernity has brought in its train, thealogy can be said to belong to a definitely modern history of religious ideas dating from the eighteenth-century Enlightenment. Howard Eilberg-Schwartz has argued that feminist witchcraft—a key grouping within the Goddess movement—does not entirely repudiate the Enlightenment project but may, indeed, be one of its products. He argues that feminist witches' criticism of modernity is turning the Enlightenment philosophers' rationalistic and emancipatory criticism of the Church's manipulative authority over the minds of the people against the Enlightenment's *own* destructive cult of rationality (1989: 77-95).

Even in their search for a new and, in some senses, post-traditional religious identity, Goddess feminists are modern in their demystification of and critical hostility to the old authoritarian, patriarchal religious traditions. In the modern fashion, Goddess feminism is looking for progress towards a utopian ideal. It enjoys the peculiarly modern possibility of religious discontinuity; what Naomi Goldenberg calls a 'changing of the gods' (1979).

As I have argued elsewhere,[11] Goddess feminism is hardly postmodern (at least in the more radical sense of the term 'postmodern') in that Goddess feminism has a powerful hope for humanity's moving beyond the 'grand narrative' or tradition of patriarchal history. To do so would not spell the end of history, but would take us into an even greater and longer 'grand narrative' or tradition of matrifocal religion. Most postmodernists would find Goddess feminist's narration of their progress towards an authentic female self and towards achieving global justice and harmony reliant on outmoded, totalizing, traditional (even quasi-biblical) ideas as well as on modern notions of human progression towards a universal, ideal historical end. Moreover, the object of the spiritual feminist quest, and perhaps its *raison d'être*, is that of the liberation of an authentic, essential, pre-patriarchal female self inhabiting a post-patriarchal planet. That such an unmediated essential self is a meaningful concept, let alone that it could be recoverable by means of particular religious practices is, from a postmodern perspective, highly questionable. There are discernible resonances here of biblical, millennial, eschatological dreams.

Goddess feminism's criticisms of modernity (especially the modern patriarchal phenomena of capitalism and technology) do not make it any the less modern itself. One of the central features of modernity is its capacity to critique all ideas and traditions—even its own. Goddess feminism, like other modern countercultural, romantic movements, is deeply anti-modern. For Goddess feminists, modernity, of all the patriarchal periods, most reveals patriarchy's disconnection from nature/femaleness and its technological 'advances' have greatly accelerated the pace of their degradation (Sjöö and Mor 1991: 405). Instead, Goddess feminism's spiritual resources are derived from an ancient, notionally pre-patriarchal Pagan past and its rituals revisit a worldview both biblical religions and modern science would call superstitious. Goddess feminism's magical

---

11. Raphael (1996c: 199-213, esp. pp. 203-207). In this paper I suggest that the late modern (rather than postmodern) features of Goddess feminism weaken its ability to do the ethically reconstructive tasks that many Goddess feminists want it to do, namely, to (re)establish a global, matrifocal, egalitarian and ecological peace within the immanent Goddess. Modernity has a critical habit of turning its knowledge of the social construction of knowledge onto its own truth claims. This has become ever more marked in late modernity. So too, as a late modern religion, thealogy's refusal to make any claim to its own authority undermines its own (earlier) modern, emancipatory elements which are absolutely morally critical of patriarchy and which have been the driving force of feminism itself.

and ecological perspective defies modern science's and industrial capitalism's view of nature as a mere machine or resource that is to be
controlled and exploited (Raphael 1997a). Countering the modern control and patriarchal abuse of technology, Goddess feminists claim that
women of the Neolithic period were the first to develop the ecologically benign technologies of cooking, ceramics, textile production, medicine, agriculture and others.

And yet despite Goddess feminism's basically modern project of moral
progress, freedom and human self-realization, it is also possible to see
Goddess feminism as, in many respects, carried upon the postmodern,
post-traditional, tide (Raphael 1996c: 199-213). Goddess religion's eclectic use of women's traditions and goddesses from a variety of the world's
religions bears many of the marks of postmodern consumer culture and
of the postmodern de-centralization and fragmentation of knowledge.
Moreover, the 'revisionary' elements of postmodern religion and philosophy which criticize modernity as a threat to natural and human
survival and which propose organic, non-mechanistic, *post*-modern conceptions of nature and its relation to the sacred are exemplified in
thealogy.[12]

Goddess religion is also typically postmodern in its refusal to authorize
its own thealogy. Rituals are conceived and performed by individuals
who make little or no claim to institutional authority. Well-known
writers like Starhawk, and Zsuszanna Budapest are simply respected and
well-loved practitioners. They may be priestesses, but they are not cult
leaders. Their style is rather to encourage other women to adapt given
rituals to their own needs and situation, or devise new ones. Indeed, the
notion of a spiritual feminist 'leader' in the normal sense of that word
would be something of a contradiction in terms. Thealogy privileges
private, local experience over formal, totalizing theory. Although it has

---

12. For an account of revisionary postmodernism see Griffin (1985: x-xi).
Raschke (1992: 100), has, however, questioned the classification of 'reconstructive'
criticism as postmodern, arguing instead that in collections such as D.R. Griffin's
Spirituality and Society: Post-Modern Visions '"postmodernism" becomes nothing more
than a buzzword for the sort of "New Age" Utopianism spun from the cerebra of
many California dreamers during the 1960s—a folio of themes and notions that are
almost now a generation out of date'. Raschke believes that 'serious [that is, post-
structuralist] postmodernism has not left its stamp on religious thought' (1992: 98)
and would presumably say the same of Goddess feminism which shares much of the
territory of revisionary 'postmodernism'.

'big theories' about patriarchy and about world history, it will not theorize the Goddess in advance of particular women's experience.

In sum, it is as if thealogy occupies an interesting boundary territory: that of the time between times. It promises a post-patriarchal future that is at the same time something of a return to a pre-patriarchal past. This occupying a time between times creates certain tensions in the thealogical project. As we will see in Chapter 3 of this study, thealogians give a (traditional and modern) reading of history as a single story of massive change that moves from global happiness to the tragedy of patriarchy, and onward to future possibilities of post-patriarchal happiness once more. And yet Goddess feminism's (postmodern) *laissez faire* approach to the production of thealogy could be to the detriment of its intellectual and religious coherence and the fulfilment of its own promise as a movement for change in the twenty-first century.

Chapter Two

The Goddess

What if, when you take the sexism out of God language, you have nothing left? What then? (Morton 1985: 223)

We women are going to bring an end to God. As we take positions in government, in medicine, in law, in business, in the arts, and, finally, in religion, we will be the end of Him. We will change the world so much that He won't fit in any more. I found this thought most satisfying (Goldenberg 1979: 3).

In the early 1970s Naomi Goldenberg's exhilaration at the Second Wave of feminism that was breaking over American culture led her to believe that the Western model of God would be made redundant by the women's revolution. But Goldenberg's confident prediction that 'We are about to learn what happens when father-gods die for a whole generation' (1979: 37) has only very partially been fulfilled. Certainly, post-Christian feminists are attempting to eradicate the patriarchal God from their consciousness and Christian feminists are developing new emancipatory models of God based on women's past and present experience and on new interpretations of biblical and theological texts. But biblical models of God as Lord, King and Father have developed over thousands of years and mainstream religious communities were not likely to accept a comprehensive reconstruction of their model of God within a couple of decades.

In fact, 17 years after the publication of *Changing of the Gods*, most female rabbis and priests tend to be moderately rather than militantly feminist and, for the sake of peace within their congregations, find themselves able to make only minor adjustments to the received patriarchal model of God held by the great majority of their congregants. In the academy and within progressive communities, reformist Jewish and

Christian feminism (especially its bid for inclusive language) has undoubtedly made itself felt, but its female images of God—despite, or
perhaps *because of* their paradigm-shifting significance—remain marginal
to 'mainstream' theology and religious practice.[1] Although it is still too
early to assess the full impact of women priests in the Anglican Church,
there is evidence from the longer experience of women ministers from
the Free Churches that widespread gender stereotyping and discrimination persists despite women's equal access to the ministry (Graham
1995: 48).

Thealogy's account of the Goddess, by nature of its radical departures,
makes even less impact on the mainstream academy and faith communities. However, given the overlap of thealogical interests and practices
with those of feminist theology and spirituality, the green movement,
the neo-Pagan revival, lesbianism, and Jungian psychotherapy, the
countercultural impact of the Goddess has been considerable and looks
set to grow.

The Plurality and Fluidity of Thealogy

Most Goddess women refer to the Goddess as *the* Goddess; as if she is
one and as if thealogians were unanimous in their concept of her. This is
not, however, the case, and concepts of the Goddess differ from person
to person and have shifted slightly even over the short space of time that
women have thealogized. In the mid-1970s, when Goddess feminism
began to emerge as a distinct element of the women's liberation movement, the term 'Goddess' functioned as what Asphodel Long has termed
'a synonym for a woman with newly regained self-worth'. Long notes
that, at this time, the term was essentially a way of liberating and
affirming the divinity of femaleness from the mediation and control of
patriarchal religion. This early period of Goddess feminism was more
interested in the psychological and political effects of adopting a heretical religious and political position than in posing metaphysical thealogical questions for itself. In her teaching and practice of Goddess religion,
Long still finds that women only raise the question of the ontological
status of the Goddess when they are 'well advanced into Goddess culture

---

1.   This may be more true of Britain than, say, Sweden, where, according to
Monica Sjöö in a letter to *From the Flames* 13 (1994): 18, women priests in mainstream communities speak freely of the Mother-God and use alternative, inclusive
prayers, hymns and rituals.

and action and are interested in debate on the subject. It actually bothers very few seekers' (1994: 15).

As we shall see, thealogy appears to have become, not more philosophically inclined, but more confident in asserting the 'real' external existence of the Goddess. Despite the increasing realism of thealogy, its lack of authoritative sacred texts enables it to remain non-dogmatic and non-credal (Weaver 1989: 50). Although Goddess feminists do have some conceptions of the nature of the Goddess, such conceptions are often implicit rather than stated and remain fluid and non-normative. So much so, that this chapter cannot simply enumerate a set of distinct models of the Goddess associated with influential writers and practitioners.

Goddess feminism is markedly anti-authoritarian, but thealogians do, nonetheless, have their own distinct emphases. Some non-realist thealogians, of the early period of Goddess feminism especially, emphasize the psychic, political or metaphoric power of the Goddess, while others, in the present especially, tend more towards thealogical realism (that is, treating the Goddess as a divinity having a real existence separate from that of the women who invoke her and to whom some or all thealogical language literally applies). Some (like Sjöö) emphasize the Mother aspect of the Goddess, while others (like Long) want to minimize the connections between Goddess religion and maternity (Harvey 1997: 76). What is significant about thealogy as a discourse is that no thealogian insists on the exclusive truth of her own perspective(s). Contemporary thealogy offers Goddess feminists a shifting collage of images of the Goddess, none of which is finally truer than another.

The Goddess can be defined so broadly that thealogical inclusivity is guaranteed. In the late 1970s Starhawk, Goddess religion's best-known priestess/thealogian, made the now well-known observation that her thealogy is contingent on her own state of being:

> It all depends on how I feel. When I feel weak, she is someone who can help and protect me. When I feel strong, she is the symbol of my own power. At other times I feel her as the natural energy in my body and the world (Christ and Plaskow 1992: 278-79).

Whether Starhawk's thealogy shifts with her mood, or the nature of the Goddess herself shifts with Starhawk's 'mood', is, perhaps deliberately, left unclear. Thealogy dislikes exclusive either/or dilemmas, finding power in the more inclusive mysterious ambiguities of both/and. Starhawk's position is typical of most Goddess women when she writes, 'I have spoken of the Goddess as psychological symbol and also as manifest reality. She is both. She exists, *and* we create Her' (1979: 81).[2] The line between the individual woman and the Goddess—as both the symbol and the divine power of femaleness—is not fixed, if it is there at all. In feminist Wicca the priestess invokes the presence of the Goddess from her own self. At that moment she *is* the Goddess.

Goddess feminism (in its more postmodern posture) is individualistic and pragmatic, believing that only as such can it serve women. Thealogians make no bid for academic prestige. Indeed, they are in agreement that as soon as thealogy sets itself up as a closed intellectual system it will cease to be iconoclastic and will become just another competing claim to truth. Caitlín Matthews urges her readers to frame their own thealogy. In 'finding a myth of the Goddess to live by', there is 'only one criteria in such a choice: *does it work for you?*' For 'the rule of the Goddess is that there is no rule'. Each woman finds the Goddess in her own experience (1989: 18-19).

Goddess feminists prefer to talk about experience rather than belief, for belief can imply a merely rational decision to affirm that something is the case. Thealogy is not, however, an intellectual project, but a process of religious self-discovery and expression that is situated in the body and in nature. Goddess feminists do not wish to sever discourse about the Goddess from discourse about themselves. Much of thealogy's attraction resides in its power to disrupt the complacencies of tradition. Goddess women would, therefore, resist the establishment of a thealogical tradition which, by its nature, would stand over and against the individual woman or block her creative flow.

Naomi Goldenberg is both an atheist and a thealogian, that is, for her, the Goddess need not be 'real' to be politically and psychologically necessary to the liberation of women. For Goldenberg, women gain freedom and maturity by leaving Judaism and Christianity behind; a departure that requires 'growing out of' dependence on 'real' external divinities, and accepting that all gods and goddesses, including the Goddess, are psychological forces or archetypes, but which are not, on that account, any less real and powerful in their effects. For witches, just

---

2.   Starhawk claims that the Goddess is 'about choosing an attitude: ... choosing to see the world, the earth, and our lives as sacred' (1990a: 11). This attitude is common to all thealogy, but it seems clear from Starhawk's body of work as a whole that she understands the Goddess far less minimally than as the symbol of an attitudinal stance.

thinking and willing the reality of the Goddess is enough to make her real. For in Wicca, 'any thought or fantasy [is] real to the degree that it influences actions in the present' (Goldenberg 1979: 42-43, 89).[3] Each woman *makes* the Goddess real by allowing the Goddess archetype to do its transformatory work through her own liberated consciousness. Not only Naomi Goldenberg, but also Carol Christ (in her earlier writing), Mary Daly and Nelle Morton understand the Goddess as a metaphor for the depth/divinity of the transformed feminist self in erotic or biophilic connection with everything that lives. As Heide Göttner-Abendroth expresses it, the concept of the Goddess signifies the inherent and integrated spiritual, intellectual, emotional and physical capacities of the individual.

> The Goddess does not exist independent of those capacities; she is some-thing like the unifying thread, the vitality, the energy of life. In this sense the Goddess is present in every person and in all creatures and elements that possess or impart the vital energy. (1991: 217)

Daly's understanding of the Goddess as a 'Verb' rather than a static noun that merely replaces the noun 'God' has made an important contribution to the non-realist elements in thealogy. For Daly, the Goddess is not just God with a sex-change:

> Goddess-images—in so far as these inspire creative activity, Self-Realizing bonding with Other women . . . —can function as Metaphors of Meta-morphosis, as verbs fostering participation in the Verb Be-ing. In these instances, Goddess Names active participation in Powers of Be-ing (1985: xviii-xix).

The nature of metaphor as that which 'carries beyond' (Greek, *meta*, after/beyond and *pherein*, carry) suggests to Daly that, as a metaphor (among a number of other such metaphors) the Goddess, like a flying broomstick, propels women out of the patriarchal state of being into a new time and space of feminist existential self-realization. Where the primordial event of patriarchal rule is 'the murder/dismemberment of the Goddess—that is, the Self-affirming be-ing of women', the radical

---

3.   This view that Goddess *power* is real, regardless of whether she is an actual deity or 'only' an unconscious archetype, is a common one. However, Conway (1994: 24-25) states that practice has shown her that magic is more likely to be efficacious when one believes in the Goddess as a deity and 'has felt the fringes of her awesome power'. For her the Goddess 'resides on another plane of existence and will help those who learn how to reach and call upon Her'.

feminist 'sin' against patriarchy becomes 'refusal to collaborate in this killing and dismembering of our own Selves as the beginning of re-membering the Goddess—the deep Source of creative integrity in women' (Daly 1991: 111).

So for some thealogians the Goddess is relatively abstract and func-tions *for them* as an emancipatory metaphor or emblem of dynamic cosmic, personal and political energies, the organic relations between all living things within the cosmos, and the divinity of female being. But for other thealogians the Goddess can *also* be a self-existent female deity with many aspects or hypostases. Thealogy can be at once non-theistic, monotheistic and polytheistic. Although most thealogians refer to the Goddess as *the* Goddess, some prefer to experience her as a life-changing symbol and some see her as that *and* a divinity in her own right. Whether as an idea or as a real divinity, or something in between, the Goddess can be experienced in and through the many names of the historically and geographically diverse goddesses. Some women adopt an ancient goddess or aspect of the Goddess that embodies the values and characteristics most relevant to them at a particular stage of their life. (The use of world mythology is not, however, indiscriminate. In Carol Christ's view, war goddesses like Ishtar and Athena are not liberative for women today; where goddesses are 'Takers of Life' they must also be 'Givers of Life' or thealogy will degenerate into a celebration of the bloodthirsty and the demonic [1987: 80, 176].)

Even within one grouping, Goddess feminists can hold diverse views. Within Dianic Wicca, some women perceive the Goddess as an inter-ventionary power to whom one can pray for miraculous assistance, while others perceive her power as manifest through finite individuals; that she is as powerful as the woman or women through whom she works (Alba 1993: 14-15). The thoroughly plural nature of thealogy does not mean that thealogians are intellectually or religiously incom-petent. Academic theology is itself highly plural and accepts—even celebrates—paradoxical or apparently self-contradictory claims about God. Non-realism has also had an important part to play in theology over the last few decades.

Yet unlike the immutable God of classical theism, the Goddess's 'con-stant theme' is, as Tanya Luhrmann writes, 'cyclicity and transforma-tion . . . Every face of the Goddess is a different goddess, and yet also the same, in a different aspect, and there are different goddesses for dif-ferent years and seasons of one's life' (1994: 48-49). That is, like other pagan goddesses and gods, the contemporary Goddess is a shape-shifter. She forms and re-forms with the shifting consciousness and changing physiological states of those who live in and through her. The meaning of the Goddess is identical with the meaning of being alive. Starhawk declares that 'All that lives (and all that is, lives), all that serves life, is Goddess' (1992: 263). And because nothing that is alive is changeless, all life is in process and motion. So, paradoxically, all that is constant about the Goddess is that she is ever-changing.

Goddess feminism celebrates the natural flux of organic life as the form and function of divine activity. As such, its thealogy is intolerant of any kind of discursive fixing: nature/the Goddess and discourse itself are in flux by virtue of being living, organic forms whose processes cannot be mapped out in advance. Neither thealogical models of the Goddess nor thealogians themselves have any pretensions to omnipotence or omniscience (though Goddess feminists—especially Wiccans—often claim psychic powers). Both thealogical discourse and nature/the Goddess represent complex, undetermined, ever-emergent patternings and dissolutions (Caputi 1993: 288-90; Raphael 1996b: 220-61).

So too, Starhawk's recent science-fiction novel, *The Fifth Sacred Thing*, suggests that the Goddess is neither personal nor impersonal; neither interventionary nor non-interventionary; neither a comforting nor indifferent deity. In the novel, a green, Pagan (but pluralistic) community is attacked by the 'Stewards' who rule the nightmarish ecocidal regime that neighbours its land. During her struggle against the Stewards, the Goddess feminist heroine, Madrone, recalls that 'one of the names of the Goddess was All Possibility', and she fleetingly wishes 'for a more comforting deity, one who would at least claim that only the good possibilities would come to pass'. And yet the 'Goddess of all Possibilities' renounces any desire for or claim to powers of determination, whispering as a voice in her ear, 'All means all . . . I proliferate, I don't discriminate. But you have the knife. I spin a billion, billion threads, now, cut some, and weave with the rest' (1994: 207).

Thealogy is a product of religious feminism's criticism of patriarchal theology. As such, thealogy has a tendency to overstate its case against the God of Jewish and Christian theology. Thealogy presents an often parodic, more or less uniform, account of God as a disembodied masculine sky god, detached from (or transcendent to) the natural cycles he created, demanding absolute obedience from his creatures, and leading history towards a pre-determined purpose in which the disobedient will be punished down in the fiery bowels of the earth and the obedient rewarded by sharing heaven with himself. The radical feminist image of the biblical God is often an oversimplification (as is Mary Daly's famous syllogism, 'if God is male then the male is God' [1985: 19]). Thealogy tends to ignore theology at its immanental best (the Christian God is, after all, intended as a God of love, incarnate on earth in the suffering flesh of Jesus and the Jewish God is present in his Torah). Thealogy's view of theology is derived from the latter's transcendental and ascetic excesses and forgets its great diversity.

Nonetheless, theology's monotheistic concentration and centralization of cosmic power in one personal, law-giving will characterized as male, is enough to make some thealogians wary of succumbing to what Emily Culpepper has called 'the inertia of monotheism' (1991: 153). Thealogy has no desire to simply reproduce the patriarchal God's solitary divine sovereignty in a female form. As Goddess feminists often claim, they do not want a 'God in a skirt'; they do not worship 'God's wife'. One self-existent female divinity would, by implication, arrogate the divinity of individual woman to herself.

For this and other reasons, Graham Harvey argues that Goddess-talk should be polytheistic and that 'it might be easier if people consistently said "Goddesses", and an increasing number do'. But whether the Goddess is invoked in the singular or plural, Harvey's view is that,

> all the Goddesses exist and are cordial enough not to be insulted if another Goddess is thanked for help. All the Goddesses co-operate in divine activities and are happy to be summed up as a community under the label 'Goddess' (1997: 167; see also Long 1997: 13-29).

Although contemporary Western Paganism is more often understood to be loosely monotheistic: the Goddess and the God are personifications of the one Divine Reality or Power (Pagan Federation 1992: 3-4), Goddess feminists' opinion on whether thealogy is properly monotheistic or polytheistic is divided. Cynthia Eller finds that genuinely polytheistic spiritual feminists, believing in a number of discrete goddesses rather than one Goddess with many names, are a rarity (1993: 133). Margot Adler, however, argues that Paganism's intrinsic polytheism makes it more tolerant than other religions and reflects how people actually think about divinity. Dianic Wiccan monotheism, she claims, is an exception in the Pagan movement, not the rule (Adler 1986: 24-38). The debate over the Goddess as one or many is not one that can or needs to be resolved here, though Carol Christ suggests a form of compromise conception that would, I think, satisfy most:

> We need 'the Goddess' as an affirmation of an intuition of the unity of being underlying the multiplicity of life. And we need a multiplicity of 'Goddesses' (and Gods) to fully reflect our differences and to remind us of the limitations of any single image (1997: 112).

Whether a thealogy is monotheistic or polytheistic it would, nonetheless, insist that authentic sacred power is not 'power-over' derived from the one divinity that has power over all else, but rather, 'power-from-within' or 'power-for' (Starhawk 1987: 14-16). Neither the Goddess nor thealogians wish to yield power over women through law or theory respectively. Thealogical method and content is intentionally imaginative, holistic, intuitive and artistic. It is not a discipline. To establish a thealogical orthodoxy would not only confine the imagination, it would grant women intellectual and social power over one another. It would create an orthodox 'us' and a heterodox 'them'.

A distinctive feature of thealogy is precisely its attempt to overcome the divisive dualities of good/evil, nature/culture, spirit/flesh, I/Not-I. Carol Christ claims that the old theological categories and binary oppositions no longer *work* in thealogical discourse and thealogy must find new ways of thinking about the divine (1997: 101). For most thealogians, the symbol/idea/reality of the Goddess overcomes these dualities because she is the dynamic interconnection, interaction and interdependence—a manifold 'constellation of forms and associations' of all that is alive (Starhawk 1990a: 9).

The inherent fluidity of thealogy can, in fact, make it as abstract and elusive as philosophical theology. This does not mean that thealogy attaches any value to abstraction per se or that it is merely a rational system of thought abstracted from life as lived, but, rather, that Goddess is (like any divinity whose presence and power is believed to encompass all being) both natural and more than just the sum of nature's parts and that her 'over-plus' of meaning is a mystery that cannot be comprehended by reason alone.

Postmodern theorists argue that social knowledge is partly or wholly an ideological construct, mediated and shaped by the interests of those who articulate it. Likewise, thealogians would claim that theology's knowledge of the divine as God is ideologically determined by the Churches and the academy who lend authority to an elite to speak on behalf of the patriarchal establishment and its interests. Goddess feminism, recognizing that knowledge is relative, attempts to thealogize without imposing its authority on others (though clearly some practitioner–thealogians like Starhawk and Zsuzsanna Budapest are especially respected and regularly quoted). If one woman claimed that her model of the Goddess was more accurate or true a model than another's that would be divisive and alienating in every sense. And yet the whole point of all religious feminism is to reunite femaleness and divinity, which patriarchy, in postulating a male, transcendent god, has set apart. Not surprisingly then, many thealogians are suspicious of transcendent deities even when they are female. The common identity of the individual woman and the Goddess entails that no divine authority stands over and against the individual who must own and name their sacrality. It was for this reason that Joan Mallonee was unwilling to write down the revelations of the Goddess she had received in dreams. She was apprehensive that

> the material would evolve into a dogma, a theology. I had a strong desire to speak about the images which were so strong and powerful, so individual and personal, but I had no desire to create the implication that She would be the same for others as She was for me (quoted in Christ 1978: 277).

Some thealogians write from more urgent feminist convictions than others.[4] Although the whole Goddess movement could be said to propose a 'family' of thealogies, thealogy is, at root and at best, a feminist project. And it is vitally important to recognize thealogy's political, strategic positioning within the context of radical religious feminism. It is this political nature of the project that guarantees fluidity in thealogy's

---

4.   V. MacIntyre [Vron] argues that 'the concept of "goddess" has become rather adopted and co-opted by non-feminists and too attached to "femininity" and/or "the Feminine Principle" which seem to me to be just more tired old patriarchal traps. This makes it harder for us as radical feminists to communicate using the concept of "goddess" without having to keep explaining what we *don't* mean' (1993: 34). So too, Daly refers to the 'New Age' style 'Goddess spirituality' that has 'massively passivising effects' and dampens the 'Radical Impulse' (1993: 208). She is presumably making a reference to Goddess worshippers who practice in mixed Pagan groups where the male God has a significant religious function and complements the attributes of the Goddess. I have included such writers in this study, but only if they also make recognizably feminist critical claims about the damaging role of patriarchy in religion and culture.

concept of the Goddess. For *whatever* one's concept of the ontological relationship between Goddess and woman and Goddess and world, even to *say* and *use* the word Goddess is politically redemptive or emancipatory. In her last public speech the late Nelle Morton urged her audience to at least try to use the word 'Goddess', even if just for a while and to dare to experience what it felt like to experience the discomfort, shock or iconoclastic force generated by its profound unfamiliarity (Keller 1998: 62). Catherine Keller adds as a gloss on Morton's address: 'The politics of the Goddess converge with the politics of metaphor itself, as a creative affront to the fixities of cosmic paternalism and all of its autocratic attempts to block the open journey' (1998: 62).

It has become clear that thealogians may hold plural conceptions of the Goddess and that their conceptions or ideas move with the ebb and flow of experience. Thealogy is properly, for Carol Christ, as for all others, a coming together of 'the voice of experience and the voice of reflection'; a product of lived, embodied struggle (1997: xvi-xvii). Indeed, this process can be traced in Carol Christ's own work, where thealogy has shifted from a concept of the Goddess as archetype to her latest more realist, theistic conception of the Goddess as 'the power of intelligent embodied love that is the ground of all being' (1997: xv); a power with whom she is in relationship. This thealogy was granted to her by a sense of the all-encompassing presence of a matrix of love that was revealed to her upon her mother's death (1997: 38).

Despite the inherent plurality and fluidity of thealogy, the reader need not despair of reaching a relatively clear idea of what the Goddess can be, and certainly of what the Goddess is not. Thealogical discourse does, and must, have distinguishing features, such that one can identify statements, arguments and texts as 'thealogy' at all. Although the purpose of thealogy is to make 'conversation about women's spirituality . . . deeper and more meaningful' (Christ 1978: 278), rather than to systematize a set of religious experiences, all Goddess feminists would more or less agree with the three following claims.

First, all Goddess feminists would agree that the Goddess *is* nature, though she is more than the sum of nature's parts. The earth is the Goddess's body, or she is at least immanent (indwelling) in the 'female' energies of cosmic, natural and social regeneration. Secondly, although, as we shall see, some thealogy is fairly conventionally realist, the Goddess is *at least* a symbol of the collective and individual 'womanpower' which is itself part of the generative power of nature. And thirdly, there would also be basic agreement that the Goddess is not simply an object of faith, in whom one might believe in spite of doubt or evidence to the contrary. Goddess feminists do not trust or *hope* that the Goddess exists; in some senses, she *is* existence and is therefore available to immediate, self-authenticating, *present* experience. As Starhawk insists in all her writing, 'She is here. She is within us all.' The reality of the Goddess is inseparable from the reality of the self; she *is* the process and the fulfilment of the 'natural' or meta-patriarchal self reborn through feminist consciousness.

Towards a Self-Existent Goddess

Despite thealogy's reluctance to set up one normative image of one Goddess over and against all private imagining, and despite its feeling that attempts to prove the existence of the Goddess would crucially miss all the political points thealogy wants to make, the Goddess is not always 'reduced' to a projection derived from feminists' new affirmation of the value of femaleness. Cynthia Eller seems right in observing that 'most spiritual feminists grant the goddess a much more substantial existence than one of concept, symbol, or linguistic device' (1993: 141). This quality of being 'more' than a psychological archetype or a political banner under which to rally women, is often signalled by capitalizing feminine pronouns for the Goddess and specifying the Goddess as *the* Goddess. Although thealogy written by academics has tended towards non-realist accounts of the Goddess as symbol, archetype or Dalyan metaphor (see Clack 1995: 104-106), I have recently argued that a realist monotheism—an account of the Goddess as one unitary, self-existent divinity—is increasingly common in all types of thealogical discourse (Raphael 1999). For the majority of Goddess feminists, the Goddess is a symbol of the emergence and legitimacy of female power (Christ 1992: 273-87), but she is *also* a divinity separate from the self and revealed through the workings of the inner self in dreams, shamanic trance states, Tarot readings, pathworking and heightened pre-menstrual awareness. The Goddess is usually, then, more than just a psychotherapeutic device for raising self-esteem and self-confidence, even though that is a highly significant and valuable *effect* of Goddess feminism.

Realist claims about the Goddess are not hard to find. As D.J. Conway puts it, 'Personally, I find the Goddess very real, not something conjured from wish-fulfilment or imagination. When one has received very explicit directions from Her in a dream that is not a dream, one no longer questions Her reality' (1994: 5). Or again, for Christ, the Goddess is personal and relational:

> When I speak the name of the Goddess, I believe I come into relationship with a power who cares about my life and the fate of the world. The more I sing to the Goddess, pray to her, and invoke her name in my daily life, the more certain this conviction becomes (1997: 104).

For De-Anna Alba, a Dianic Wiccan, the Goddess is quite clearly a separate divine agent:

> Although I know the Goddess dwells in me and works through me, I do not and cannot contain the totality of what She is and what She knows . . . I trust Her to know and do what is best, even if I cannot see it at the time. I am Her child and like any mother She has my best interests at heart. (1993: 19)

The sense of the Goddess as a real divinity external to the self does not simply replay some of the more facile elements of older interventionist theologies. In Starhawk's novel *The Fifth Sacred Thing*, Bird and Madrone —the novel's two main protagonists (and to a large degree, vehicles of her own thealogy)—discuss the possibility of divine deliverance from evil. Bird remembers an experience of deliverance from evil, but not by 'an old guy with a beard, and it wasn't a big lady in the sky. But . . . something did reach for me':

> I'm trying to say that *this*, this livingness we're all in and of, has something in it that reaches for freedom. Maybe that quality isn't first or most central. It could be just like a single thin thread buried in a whole carpet. But it's there. The outstretched hand is there. If you reach for it, it'll grab you back (1994: 215).

During the struggle against the twenty-first century brutal necrophilic regime of the Stewards that the novel narrates, the Goddess is present (though not invariably) in the consciousness of those who invoke her and in natural 'signs' like swarms of bees or tides that bring help or safety to the novel's main protagonists. At the end of the novel the Steward's regime is not destroyed forever (as it might have been in patriarchal futuristic fiction), but the ecofeminist community Madrone and Bird have worked to establish keeps the Stewards at bay by peaceful means and looks set to survive into the foreseeable future. In other words, thealogy might not envisage the Goddess simply directing historical events by continual benign interventions, but neither does it perceive the cosmos as empty of a life-affirming will and presence.

A factor that drives towards thealogical realism lies in Goddess feminism's bid to reclaim the Goddess from patriarchal history. Some Goddess feminists—particularly those interested in the Western goddess heritage—have wanted to say that Paganism has always assumed the existence of the one Great Goddess as a unitary divine agent with many names. In establishing a historical continuity between the contemporary revival of the Goddess and the Great Goddess/Mother of the deep past, thealogy bestows a coherent, continuous presence upon Goddess religion and a potentially global meaning and purpose upon the revival. As Merlin Stone claims,

> Ashtoreth, the despised "pagan" deity of the Old Testament was actually . . . Astarte—the great Goddess, as She was known in Canaan, the near Eastern Queen of Heaven . . . elsewhere known as Innin, Innana, Nana, Nut, Anat, Anahita, Istar, Isis, Au Set, Ishara, Ashera, Astart, Attoret, Attar and Hathor—the many-named Divine Ancestress. Yet each name denoted, in the various languages and dialects of those who revered Her, the Great Goddess (1976: 9).[5]

Stone, like other historically inclined spiritual feminists, claims that the close transnational similarities among the titles, images and symbols of the Goddess, the annual death and mourning cycles for the Goddess's consort, the institutions of eunuch priests and the annual sacred sexual unions between the Goddess and her divine consort or son, 'all reveal the overlapping and underlying connections between the worship of the female deity in areas as far apart in space and time as the earliest records of Sumer to classical Greece and Rome' (Stone 1976: 23; Adler 1986: 229). So although radical religious feminism may want to sever its links with patriarchal religion, it does not necessarily want to renounce its claim to a major Western—even monotheistic—tradition.

Western monotheism tends to be personalistic and Goddess feminism, for all its protestations against monotheism, is not immune to the attractions of personifying the Goddess or using personal language to describe her. It is, after all, difficult for a religion to produce mythology, ritual

---

5.   King notes that thealogians do not make the customary distinctions made by historians of religion between the Great Goddess and the Great Mother, the latter being a fertility Goddess of the Earth and the former being a metaphysical principle of the Oneness of reality who therefore transcends biology. Undoubtedly thealogians see the Goddess as both the Great Mother and the Great Goddess. But King is suspicious of the elevation of biological motherhood to a transcendental status that such a fusion implies (1989: 148-49).

and art without personifying its divinities to some degree. At a recent sunrise ritual to the Sun Goddess on the top of Glastonbury Tor, I was struck by the manner in which requests were made and thanks offered to the Goddess. From my perspective as a participating observer, the ritual suggested a real interventionary female divinity who would respond to what sounded very much like petitionary prayers.

Again, thealogy's wanting to say that nature is not *like* a mother, but really *is* the Mother, has spawned a number of mythological images of the earth having been birthed from the Goddess's own, real body, as in the following cosmogony by Charlene Spretnak:

> From the eternal Void, Gaia danced forth and rolled Herself into a spinning ball . . . from Her warm moisture She bore a flow of gentle rain that fed Her surface and brought life. Wriggling creatures spawned in tidal pools, while tiny green shoots pushed upwards through her pores. She filled oceans and ponds and set rivers flowing through deep furrows (Spretnak and Capra 1985: 5-6; see also Cameron 1985: 54-56).

Thealogical cosmology will tend to imply that the Goddess is what we are but is also real and external to us just as is nature which is both what we are and the tangible external environment that brings us into being.

In addition to this inherent cosmological realism, Goddess feminists can even experience a sense of mission, of having been called by the Goddess to a task they might not have chosen. In ways comparable to a Christian receiving a 'call' from God, Malka Golden Wolfe, a feminist from Arizona, experienced a 'call' from the Goddess 27 years ago. The Goddess asked Wolfe to introduce her to the many radical feminists of the 1970s who were not aware of her existence and presence. The Goddess told Wolfe to say of her 'I will not be ignored—this is my time. Heal my body . . . I have wisdom to share.' Now post-menopausal and having the status of a Crone, Wolfe has been called by the Goddess to 'go to the old women'. This call has led to Wolfe's present work with the Council of Crones and Grandmothers (a network of groups which support older women's struggle for a social and political voice and to celebrate the process of their ageing in the Goddess).[6]

Nelle Morton too, although a keen advocate of the metaphoric power of the Goddess also recounts moments in which the Goddess could only

---

6. Taken from Wolfe's introduction to the work of the International Council of Crones and Grandmothers, The Goddess Conference, Glastonbury, August 9 1997. For other accounts of 'revelations' of the Goddess from feminist writers see e.g. Christ (1987: 191); Tate (1997a: 2-3; 1997b: 8).

be described as a real presence (1985: 150, 162). However, as in theology, personalistic language for the Goddess should not be taken too literally or as an exhaustive account of the nature of the Goddess. She is (like God) both personal and non-personal. A typical evocation of the Goddess as a divinity whose nature is at once personal/abstract and private/cosmic is that given by De-Anna Alba:

> Goddess is everywhere, within and without. She is in our innermost thoughts and in our wildest imaginings. She sits at the center of the universe and enfolds it to Her breast. She is in the Earth under our feet, in the air we breathe and in the water we drink. The spark of Her essence ignites our passions, whether they be sexual, social, political or spiritual in nature. She animates mammals, reptiles and amphibians. She enlivens the plant world and imparts Her substance to minerals. She is as close as our heartbeat and is rooted in our wombs. She is as distant as the furthest star. She is all (1993: 11-12).

Speaking for Dianic Wiccans, Alba affirms the transcendence as well as the immanence of the Goddess. Noting that this is not a subject Dianics actually discuss very much, she writes,

> Not only is the Goddess within us, She is "out there" too—amongst the stars in deep space. Many invocations I've heard (and written) speak of this. When we invoke the Goddess we look up at the sky or ceiling, or at least tilt the head up slightly. If we truly felt She existed only within us, we would only be looking at our wombs when we invoke Her. If She is only a Goddess of the Earth (i.e., nature) we should be looking at the ground or the floor. But we don't (1993: 14).

Alba goes on to say that the Dianic invocation of the Goddess with slightly raised and opened arms signals the transcendence of the Goddess; her being is 'differently located', though not withdrawn or separated from humanity. With a claim not unlike that customarily made by theologians about the relation of God's immanence to his transcendence, Alba writes that the Goddess is 'the Sacred Other who is yet at one with us and connected to us, whose totality of being extends beyond our Earth-related and individual perceptions of Her' (1993: 14).

The Triple Goddess

Imaging the Goddess as a triune deity is most typical of feminist witchcraft, but is no means exclusive to witches. Most thealogians insist that 'from the earliest ages, the Great Goddess was conceived as a trinity and was a model for all subsequent trinities, female, male or mixed' (Walker

1983: 1018). As patriarchy became ever more deeply rooted in human consciousness, Goddess feminists agree that triple Goddesses such as the Greek Hebe-Hera-Hecate were to be replaced by all-male trinities such as the Christian Trinity of Father, Son and Holy Spirit,[7] and the Germanic Pagan trinity of Woden, Thor and Saxnot.

The classical Christian Trinity is, arguably, triangular; although orthodox Christianity regards the three persons of the Trinity as co-equal and indivisible, in effect, the Son and the Holy Spirit often appear subordinate to and in some senses derived from the Father. By contrast, the thealogical trinity is fully circular. In the Triple Goddess, the three aspects of Maiden, Mother and Crone are comparable to the waxing, full and waning phases of the moon; no one aspect is subordinate to another and each aspect passes into the other within one dynamic, swirling, repeating and yet never-the-same circle. The Triple Goddess is not a feminized version of the Christian Trinity. Imaging the Goddess as Maiden, Mother and Crone draws all transformations—material and spiritual—into the divine/natural economy. For humanity, the Triple Goddess represents a comprehensive revaluation of each woman or man's physiological, psychological and political development and change. Contrary to oft-repeated liberal feminist criticism of the Goddess as cloyingly and retrogressively maternal, the Triple Goddess is not solely defined by motherhood, but encompasses a multiplicity of female creative (and destructive) modes. Here the sacred meanings of the female process are *sui generis* and cannot be subordinated to, or exploited by, any patriarchal project. As Naomi Goldenberg contends, 'The triple Goddess provides imagery of depth and mythic impact, which is completely unavailable to women in any other Western tradition' (1979: 98).

It must be remembered that for all Goddess feminists, the trinity of Maiden, Mother and Crone is not a strictly schematic or chronological reflection of a woman's biological life history. A woman can experience herself as Maiden, Mother or Crone at any stage or moment in her life, depending on her mood and situation. This configuration of the divine redeems the sometimes difficult transitions between such stages not only from patriarchal demonization, but also from patriarchal reduction and trivialization. Thus Shân Jayran:

---

7.   Even in patriarchal theology, the immanent presence of God can be feminized as female (Shekhinah in Judaism and the Holy Spirit in Christianity). Nonetheless, such 'feminine' attributes of God are always subordinate to the masculine.

> The Goddess is the original Trinity, Maiden, Mother, Crone. While the
> Maiden is still feted in modern consciousness as long as she's a good girl,
> the Mother has diminished to become a dutiful wife. Crones have been
> thoroughly suppressed, and replaced by little old ladies (1985: 6).

Above all, women's transformation from youth, to maturity, to old age
replicates the birthing, nurturing and regenerative activity of the Triple
Goddess. Where female biology is more or less profane in patriarchal
religions, it is now sacralized by its transposition into the changing
'body' of the Goddess as she too passes from Maiden to Mother to
Crone. For Goddess women, the Goddess is the sacred source and/or
symbol of the energies of both decay and regeneration: not only natural,
but cultural too. This means that the liberated female reproductivity of
the post-patriarchal woman is not only biological but also cultural and a
microcosm and an embodied sign of political change.

The basic characteristics of each aspect of the Triple Goddess (who is
all and each of her three aspects at once) have been lyrically imaged by
a number of writers,[8] including D.J. Conway in her book, *Maiden,
Mother, Crone*. For some Goddess feminists, Conway's thealogy might
erase too much of the moral ambiguity of the Goddess and might be a
little more monotheistic than they would prefer, but as her evocation is
recent and closely similar to many others, I have combined my own
synthesis of many accounts of the Triple Goddess with detail and quotation from hers to give what I hope is a representative picture of the
Triple Goddess in contemporary thealogy as a whole.

The Maiden (often called the Virgin or Huntress) is the first aspect of
the Goddess. As the beginning of the life cycle, she represents spring and
renewal and is traditionally associated with the colour white: 'She is the
dawn, eternal youth and vigor, enchantment and seduction, the waxing
Moon.' Through the Maiden, women can recover innocent wonder at
the beauty of nature and, in offering a fresh perspective on life, she can
be 'the Creatress of new ideas and new beginnings'. But although the
Maiden is a friend of all young creatures, she is also Huntress and 'Mistress of the Woodland'. In other words, the Maiden has a more threatening, wild, independent side. Although she never engages in mindless
destruction, she can hunt and kill. She is 'the armed keeper of the

---

8.   For summaries of the role of each hypostasis within the Triple Goddess see
e.g. Alba (1993: 6-7); Brooke (1993: 25-37); Goldenberg (1979: 97-99); Jayran
(1985: 66-71); Moorey (1997: 28-40).

Mother's universal laws, a swift messenger from the Divine Source of life and can therefore can deal out punishment to offenders of those laws, not blindly as with the figure of blind-folded Justice, but dispassionately as a guardian of balance.' In all aspects of the Triple Goddess, justice is exercised as an ecological preservation of balance. The Maiden's dispassionate justice is a function of her unattached youth and virginity. The Maiden's virginity is not physical, indeed she can revel in her sexuality. Rather, she is 'virgin' because she is independent: 'Her own person'. In human beings, the Maiden represents the stage of puberty, leading a girl to menarche and towards maturity: 'Teasing with laughter and promises, She runs before us, enticing us to follow the path we fear the most.' In world mythology, the goddesses most associated with the Maiden aspect are the Greek goddesses Kore-Persephone, Artemis and Athene, the Egyptian Neith, the Irish Danu, the Welsh Blodeuwedd, the Indian Parvati, the Finnish Mielikki, the Aztec Chimalman and many others (Conway 1994: 21-42).

As the Goddess is imaged in circular form, the Maiden phase also incorporates aspects of the Mother and Crone. The Mother aspect's colour is red, symbolizing the life force. The Mother is manifest in the ripening and fruition of all things. She is the 'high point in all cycles, whether of living or creating, for the Mother blesses and gives with open hands'. As the nurturer of creation, the Mother's love is understanding, unconditional, but not sentimental and she chastises humankind when necessary. In humans, she manifests herself as sexual, intellectual and spiritual maturity, 'She does not run before us like the Maiden, but walks beside us, hand in hand, whispering revelations and prophecies.' There are thousands of Mother goddesses throughout world mythology; Conway lists a good number of them and some of the better known names include the Greek Gaia and Demeter, the Roman Tellus Mater, the Egyptian Hathor and Isis, the Indian Durga and Sarasvati, the Chinese Kwan Yin, the Slavonic Mati Syra Zemlya and the African Mawu (1994: 45-74).

In the ferocity of her defence of her human and non-human young and her judgment upon those who abuse them, the Mother incorporates aspects of the Crone. The Crone is the most fearsome of the three aspects of the Goddess. Her colours are black, dark blue and purple. These are colours that, like the Crone, absorb all light/life into their darkness, for she represents the cauldron from which all life is tipped out and into which it will be poured back. The Crone's womb is a bubbling cosmic cauldron which recycles all life. It is therefore at once a vessel of death, creation and rebirth. As a vortex into which all categories of understanding are, like everything else, dissolved and remade, the Crone represents 'winter, night, outer space, the abyss, menopause, advancement of age, wisdom, counsel, the gateway to death and reincarnation, and the Initiator into the deepest mysteries and prophecies. The waning moon is Her monthly time of power' (1994: 77).

For Pagans, the end is also the beginning; destruction and recreation are one indivisible process. The Crone aspect leads all beings from the end of their embodied life towards their transformation into another life's new beginning (or its own reincarnation). Conway images the Crone as one who 'guides us with her lantern of ultimate truth and wisdom, not running ahead as does the Maiden, but just before us with a firm confident step', taking us through the labyrinth (the spiralling path of spiritual growth) 'on into the black void beyond the Mother' and towards the end of the labyrinth which is also its beginning. Most thealogians almost exult in the transgressive dreadfulness of the Crone aspect of the female divine and its utter refusal of feminine virtues, but Conway offers an unusually reassuring image of the Crone as one who is, like natural death, 'not to be dreaded, but welcomed. One good mental exercise to dispel fear is to meditate upon going into Her cauldron-like existence, meeting Her face to face, and feeling the love She bears for all Her creations'. So while some might imagine the Crone as a cackling hag having the last laugh on patriarchy, or as a terrifyingly dispassionate world destroyer (a way of accommodating natural suffering into a credible image of divinity), Conway tries to break that stereotypical image of the Crone aspect: 'She is not the fearsome cowled figure bearing a scythe, but rather . . . we must teach ourselves to once more see Her as She is: not annihilation, pain and perpetual suffering, but deep love, comfort, and understanding' (1994: 77-82). Well known Crone goddesses—(who might be rather less sympathetic than Conway's account of the Crone) include the Indian Kali Ma, the Egyptian Nekhbet (Mut), the Greek Hecate, the Slavonic Baba-Yaga and the Welsh Cerridwen.[9]

9. Feminist research into the Maiden, Mother and Crone goddesses whom Goddess feminists usually understand as manifestations of the one Great Mother/Triple Goddess can be pursued in texts such as Larrington (1992); Dexter (1990); Downing (1990); Koltuv (1986); Monaghan (1990); Olson (1983); Patai (1978); Shepsut (1993); Spretnak (1992); Stone (1991); Walker (1983; 1988); Wilshire (1994).

The Triple Goddess could be said to be a composite of contemporary and historical images of female divinity. However, the feminist theologian and historian of religion, Ursula King, has noted that there may be dangers in thealogy's often indiscriminate fusion of extinct and contemporary goddesses such as those from the very different cultures of Japan, Africa and India. King observes that some of the world's goddesses are 'profoundly ambivalent' and Goddess feminism has, in her view, usually given less attention to these goddesses than to the nurturant, renewing and transformatory goddesses. King reminds Goddess feminists that, 'there are also numerous goddesses of terrible demonic and destructive aspects representing the powers of darkness and death, horrible figures which are irrational, merciless and devouring' (1989: 122, 129).

However, I am not convinced that thealogians *do* want to gloss over the abysmal elements of the Goddess. The way in which the Crone aspect bestows divine meaning upon the real travail of embodied life and death is part of the very point of thealogy and, thealogically, Goddess women have strong stomachs. Goddess feminists do not, however, celebrate violence as such. While the death-dealing capacities of the Goddess are integral to our coming to terms with mortality, it would be self-contradictory for Goddess feminists to affirm the cruelty, domination and thirst for blood that characterizes some goddesses within patriarchal traditions while resisting domination and brutality in their own religio-political praxis (Christ 1997: 97-98).

Where King is right is in noting that, above all, the Goddess is not so much returning as enjoying 'a new birth and second coming'. That is, the Goddess is 'not a simple historical reconstruction, but a new creation with the help of ancient materials' (1989: 129). And as a new and continuing creation the concept of the Triple Goddess will evolve with and reflect the sensibilities of the times.[10]

10. By way of illustrating this point, it is interesting to note that in urban Hinduism the advent of American-style mass media has rendered the Mother goddess Durga (India's most popular goddess) whiter, far more placid and less elemental than she once was. She is now as made-up and bejewelled as any quasi-Hollywood heroine in an Indian film. Even Kali—Durga's fiercer incarnation—has become more serene (*Kali's Smile*, produced by T. Watt, BBC Radio 4, 13 August 1997). Similarly, there is no reason why Western Goddess feminists should be immune from projecting their own aesthetic and political values onto the models of the Goddess they inherit from the past and even from the Goddess(es) celebrated in the 1970s.

The femaleness of the Triple Goddess is in no doubt. For Dianic feminist witches, the exclusively female nature of the Triple Goddess is defended on the grounds that no single understanding of the divine is adequate for everyone and that as females gestate and feed new life, it is logical to understand the divine as female in character. For others, although the Triple Goddess is (or is imaged as) female, and women's voices and experiences are (if only temporarily) privileged, the Goddess is believed to belong to the collective memory and unconscious of *all* humankind and her celebration is not regarded as exclusive to women. Non-separatists honour the Horned God or male consort of the Goddess to a lesser or greater degree. And as importantly, most thealogians argue that the Goddess can restore spiritual balance to men: 'Her way is one of balanced living, of peaceful co-existence, of equality of sexes and races' (Conway 1994: x). Starhawk speaks for non-separatist thealogy as a whole when she writes, 'She [the Goddess] includes the male in her aspects: He becomes child and Consort, stag and bull, grain and reaper, light and dark.' To assert the primary femaleness of the Goddess is not to denigrate the masculine, but to revalue the capacity of femaleness to bring life into the world (1990a: 9).

Moreover, the femaleness of the Goddess is not literally a genital condition. The Goddess is 'female' in that she represents non- or anti-patriarchal values and activity. She is/symbolizes the generativity of the earth and is therefore 'female' in two ways. First, the being of the Goddess is Other to the instrumental rationality and exploitative politics associated with masculine, patriarchal intellectual and economic systems. Secondly, the Goddess *is* the dynamic of a cyclic, cosmic, natural process of gestation, birth, growth, decay and death which also characterizes female biology and the female activities of human and non-human animals whose lives usually participate most directly in that process. Yet it must be emphasized that the femaleness of the Goddess need not exclude pro-feminist men from Goddess religion if they wish to affirm their own capacities for nurturance and connection, and their own naturalness and mortality, by celebrating her.

This chapter has been written less for thealogians themselves than for those who are trying to understand thealogy from the outside. It has tried to clarify and define what the Goddess can be and is not within thealogical discourse. In deference to the subject, it seems appropriate to conclude this chapter on a less rationalistic note. It is not that I think rational (that is, conceptual rather than experiential) exposition of thealogy is unhelpful. Rather, it may be that the duality of an enquiring subject and an enquired-into object upon which rational exposition is conducted actually obscures both the Otherness and the identity of the divine 'object' called 'the Goddess'. Thealogy is, after all, relatively newborn and women's sense of the meaning and being of the Goddess will grow with time and experience. I suspect Mary Jo Weaver speaks for many when she concludes a paper on the revival of Goddess religion by writing of the Goddess, 'I am not sure who she is, or even if she can be named at this point' (1989: 63).

Chapter 3

Thealogy and History

Set against [the] long galactic, terrestrial and human time of *knowing* our oneness [with the cosmos and with each other], the past four thousand years of patriarchy's institutional and doctrinal *denial* of our oneness, once we see it for what it was, will appear a mere aberration. *Just a brief forgetting* (Sjöö and Mor 1991: 424).

Perhaps the most common flashpoint for controversy between spiritual feminists and other feminists occurs when the former begin to narrate the history of the Goddess and of the changing status of women: a history underpins their whole political and religious self-understanding. And it is in order not to settle this controversy but to elucidate its main elements and causes that the present chapter has been written.

Goddess religion is both a very old and a very new phenomenon. As the latest manifestation of Western Goddess religion, Goddess feminism is only about 25 years old. Compared with most other contemporary religions it is almost newborn. Yet, for Goddess feminists, their religion also has the longest history of all the world's religions. For throughout the world, the worship and symbolism of female divinity seems to have preceded the worship and symbolism of male divinity (probably because the awesome mystery of new life comes from female, not male, bodies). This means that Goddess feminism is, so to speak, everyone's and no one's past. It is a part of everyone's past because, it is believed, the patriarchal religions suppressed and destroyed the forms of Goddess religion that the world had once enjoyed. And it is no one's immediate past because, even among most surviving native traditions, patriarchy has deprived the world of its truly matrifocal Goddess heritage by repeated acts of political, religious and scholarly erasure.

Like all religions, however, contemporary Goddess religion must remember its past in order to find and celebrate its present. Identity is derived from memories, selected and organized into oral and textual histories. For a Goddess feminist to trace her historical identity is by no means straightforward as, unlike most of the world's religions, the history of Western goddess worship is a broken one.[1] From the fourth to the second millennium BCE the Mediterranean area was conquered by patriarchal tribes worshipping warrior gods like Zeus and Yahweh. Western Goddess worship finally came to an end in 348 CE when Constantine closed down the Pagan temples. Goddess religion was not to be openly revived until about 1975 CE—one and a half millennia later. This long spiritual and historical hiatus renders the content and identity of contemporary Goddess religion somewhat problematic. As Caitlín Matthews remarks,

> To whom do we go for experience of the Goddess? There are no recognised temples, professional priesthoods or sustained traditional practices stemming from the time when the Goddess was a spiritual influence upon the West (1989: 6).

However, Goddess feminists do not believe that they need to reinvent entirely their identity, for neither the Goddess nor her devotees simply vanished in the intervening years of patriarchal rule, but rather went underground—particularly after the patriarchal revolution (as it is sometimes called), after the rise of Christendom and during the witch-hunts of the fifteenth, sixteenth and seventeenth centuries. A common metaphor for the continuous presence/absence of the Goddess is that of the ceaseless passage of an underground stream. Forced beneath the surface of history, the Goddess and the practices that honoured her and nourished women and the earth, are a self-renewing, life-giving circulatory system that eventually bubbles to the surface to refresh and revive those that drink from it.

Goddess feminism claims, then, an eventful history that is at once broken and continuous. Yet it must always be borne in mind that Goddess feminists do not perceive themselves as only belonging to the ordinary linear historical continuum. For Goddess feminists, their religion

---

1.   For those outside Goddess feminism the relatively abrupt end of ancient Western goddess religion makes its history and its historical interests look rather lopsided. Malmgreen has remarked that 'those most interested in spirituality have not always been historically inclined; some contemporary feminists have spoken and written as if the tradition of women's sacred wisdom is a direct legacy from ancient (even prehistoric) times to the present—with little of consequence happening in between' (1986: 1).

represents a decisive break with history. Where 'history' is understood to refer to the (in thealogical terms, short) history of patriarchy, Goddess feminists inhabit a different—circular—temporal ambit. They at once intend a post-patriarchal religion by reclaiming its pre-patriarchal form.

Moreover, their interest in the ancient history of Goddess worship is not merely antiquarian, but political. As Merlin Stone puts it, Goddess feminists 'find [them]selves wondering to what degree the suppression of women's rites has actually been the suppression of women's rights (1976: 228). It is believed that ancient Goddess religion may provide evidence for societies where women had the kind of spiritual and cultural authority that patriarchy denied them and which spiritual feminism now seeks to restore.

Oppression and Liberation in Goddess Feminist Historical Perspective

In a much-quoted sentence, Judy Chicago has claimed of women that 'our heritage is our power; we can know ourselves and our capacities by seeing that other women have been strong' (Chicago 1982: 156). To be politically and religio-dramatically effective, the historical narrative of female power must be relayed in an abbreviated, accessible and dramatic form that has both personal and communal relevance. Its recital should, and does, function as a kind of litany whose basic elements and structure are easily learned and performed. As Cynthia Eller puts it, this history is a sacred history, that is,

> The entire cycle, from bliss to destruction to rejuvenated hope, is a narrative that functions religiously: a sacred history. It explains who we are, how we came to be, where we are going, and how to get there. In a few simple lines, one finds a thealogy, a values system, and a political agenda all interleaved. (1993: 151)

The telling of spiritual feminist history does more than give spiritual feminists an identity and a justification for calling Goddess feminism the latest form of the oldest, most widespread and one of the most oppressed of the world's religions. This sacred history is at once the history of the Goddess, of nature and of women: the suppression and liberation of all three is a unitary process. Thealogy does not conceive of the Goddess as a divine being wholly separate from the being of and becoming of women or nature. Indeed for some Goddess feminists, she has no independent subsistence at all, but names the liberated energies of

women and nature. But however one conceives of the precise ontological status of the Goddess, nature and women, the history of the oppression or liberation of one carries with it the history of the oppression or
liberation of the rest.

The rise of patriarchy as a parasitic system that prospers by taking for-
cible possession of the life energies of women, subject men and nature
to service and fuel its projects has entailed their historical control by a
male elite (and their families). The rise of patriarchy has also entailed the
eradication of those immanent female divinities whose transformatory
power fuels life and those cultures which value life *as* life, not as the
means to power. Therefore it is believed that, when patriarchy is 'over'
and the Goddess is celebrated once more, women's status will rise and,
more, produce new values and a new type of biophilic and egalitarian
social order. The consequence of liberating women/nature/the Goddess
from the patriarchal world view and its institutional structures and practices is that ecological (female) generative energies will be liberated and
once more revered. That is, the liberation of women and subject men
from patriarchy will bring about the kind of spiritual and political transformations that will heal nature's wounds and revive the divine principle
that constitutes the vitality of nature and (biophilic) human culture,
namely the Goddess. With this rebirth, history can begin anew.

The basic sacred narrative is a global one, encompassing the world's
earliest religious history. Goddess worship is believed to be humanity's
common religious heritage (Brooke 1993: 2). The narrative runs as fol-
lows. The pre-patriarchal 'matriarchal' or matrifocal Goddess-worshipping cultures can be dated from about 30,000 BCE.[2] These cultures were
peaceful, egalitarian (male and female graves seem to contain goods of
equal number and value [Gimbutas 1982: 23]), art-loving, agrarian, and
worshipped earth, sea and lunar deities. However, radiocarbon dating
shows that waves of invading Indo-European horseman/warrior tribes
from the North began their two thousand year onslaught on the
matrifocal cultures of India and Europe from approximately 2000 BCE

---

2.   Note that 'matriarchal' is a word that not all spiritual feminists believe
accurately describes pre-patriarchal culture. Many prefer to use the word 'matristic'
as indicating a non-authoritarian, matrifocal, perhaps matrilineal, community that
particularly celebrates 'female' values and characteristics. However, even where the
adjective 'matriarchal' is used, the word does not connote the tyrannous rule of
women but rather the exercise of a qualitatively different, pacific, egalitarian, spiritual power whose dynamics are always in harmony with those of nature.

(Sjöö 1992: 152). From this time, spiritual feminist archaeology notes an abrupt disappearance of the painted pottery, figurines, shrines and symbols that characterized a female religion of cyclic regeneration (Gimbutas 1982: 30). These patriarchal nomadic tribes worshipped either a young warrior god or a supreme father-god, or both together. The contrast drawn between matrifocal and patriarchal culture is a stark one. The latter was (and remains) warlike, mobile, stock-breeding, hierarchical, and its deities are generally orientated towards the transcendental symbols and spaces of mountains, sky and sun.

Goddess feminism is not, however, inclined to accept the utter vanquishment of women by patriarchy. Resistance to patriarchy by tribes of Amazons from the Mediterranean, Central Asia, Africa and South America contributes a mythological paradigm—and for some, a historical prototype—of feminist (especially lesbian separatist) power. According to D.J. Conway, the Amazons fought the advent of patriarchy, 'and thereafter, lived in exclusive female-only groups, dealing with men only for reproductive purposes. The Amazons became such effective, fierce warriors that even the Greeks grudgingly admired them' (1994: 14).

Despite its new patriarchal context, Goddess worship persisted into the classical periods of Greece and Rome, albeit undermined by revised mythologies that demoted great goddesses to wives, sisters and daughters of the gods or even had them slain. Thealogians' most common exemplar of this ancient patriarchal erasure of female divine power is that of the ancient Sumerian myth of the murder and mutilation of Tiamat, the serpent goddess of chaos by her grandson, Marduk, who usurped her power by creating the (patriarchal) world from her body. The eventual triumph of male monotheism entailed the subordination of women: 'because the deity was now exclusively male, and the Earth is obviously not his body, She was to be his handmaiden and do his bidding' (Sjöö 1992: 154). Not only was the female divine to become subservient the male divine, female divine power was to be denigrated and demonized as a merely sexual power without any social or religious authority and as being destructive or even evil if left uncontrolled by men.

Many Christian feminists claim that early Christianity was a relatively sexually egalitarian sect, especially during the period of its social marginalization and persecution. However, by about 500 CE, Christianity had moved to the powerful centre. The Christian emperors had closed down the last temples to the goddesses, and the books and mysteries of the goddess cults were being destroyed and churches built on top of their shrines. Now Western Goddess worship could only survive in vestigial forms by its transference and assimilation into the new patriarchal religion. Memories of Goddess religion were preserved in the worship of the Virgin Mary (imaged, as in pre-patriarchal representations of the Goddess, with her little son in her lap), in the Christian/Pagan syncretism which merged the identities of Christian saints and indigenous goddesses, and in healing, midwifery and witchcraft or hedge magic.

Worse was to come. The late Middle Ages and the Protestant Reformation of the early modern period were to destroy the Pagan/Catholic spirituality based upon the veneration of Mary and the female saints that had given strength and solace to women, especially in times of loss and during the stress of childbirth. The Protestant closure of the convents also deprived women of a degree of spiritual and social autonomy. But the most terrifying events of early modernity were the witch-hunts which were responsible for the murder of up to nine million women between the beginning of the fifteenth and the end of the seventeenth century.[3] That the witch-hunters singled out solitary, old, 'odd' looking or particularly sexually attractive women has bequeathed to subsequent generations of women a fear of being independent or exceptional, and of using 'old wives', remedies and rituals that were outside the prayer and healing practices of the Church (Starhawk 1990a: 183-219).

In Protestant communities, 'wilful' women could be demonized as witches or harlots. Women who were quiet and pious were sanctified as housewives and mothers, whose spiritual duties were the religious education of their young children and obedience to their husbands, whose power was to replace that of the Catholic priests and the local wise women. By the early nineteenth century the Industrial Revolution had eroded the family enterprises that had once given women a productive economic and social role. Industrialization established a gendered division between the public world of work and the private domestic sphere. Bourgeois women were confined to the latter and became leisured accessories to their husbands. Working-class women, who could not aspire to

---

3. It is widely agreed that women, rather than men, were the main targets of persecution and formed between 75 per cent and 90 per cent of the victims of the witch-hunts. Estimates for the total number of female deaths are far more contentious. Few outside spiritual feminists circles would accept that nine million women were murdered and it is commonly estimated that the witch craze took approximately 100,000 lives (Starhawk 1990a: 187).

this feminine ideal, became unpaid household drudges or had their vitality sapped by heavy domestic, agricultural or industrial labour.

While the spiritual feminist reconstruction of prehistory is peculiar to spiritual feminism itself, its historiography of the modern period clearly intersects with that of secular feminism. All feminists regard the Enlightenment period's liberal humanism and its criticism of ecclesiastical authority, tradition and superstition, as having sown the egalitarian seeds for the growth of the women's liberation movement. By 1848 'strong-minded women' (as they were known) were to assemble at the Seneca Falls Women's Rights Convention, a turning point in the development of feminist consciousness that would, eventually, bring about legal, educational and dress reform.

Moving on about 150 years from the Seneca Falls convention, the narrative begins to depart from secular feminist history and join forces with postmodern commentators who sense that history has reached a new spiritual crisis. Reconstructive postmodern spirituality, of which green and feminist spirituality are a part, is hopeful that the end of this millennium represents a period of spiritual–cognitive shift from exploitative to reverential attitudes to life. Like many others, Goddess feminists are aware of the possibility of the earth's becoming uninhabitable through nuclear wars and accidents, and a lethal cocktail of global warming, ozone depletion, resource wars and the new viruses and cancers that environmental degradation produces. The very starkness of humanity's choice between ending its history or making a new beginning is a sign of its inhabiting an end-time, or at least the end of the present phase of modernity.

As long ago as 1971 Elizabeth Gould Davis observed in the language of apocalypse: 'The ages of masculinism are now drawing to a close. Their dying days are lit up by a flare of universal violence and despair such as the world has seldom before seen' (1971: 339). The spiritual feminist narrative bears the dramatic tension of several possible outcomes. First, patriarchal pollution and weaponry could end human history by making the planet inhospitable to most species. Secondly, nature/the Goddess could end history for us by ridding herself of the human (patriarchal) parasite. Thirdly, Western(ized) humanity could respond to the organicist paradigm shift, liberate its long-suppressed Goddess-consciousness, and mend its ways in time to allow nature/the Goddess to recover her health and re-establish her own equilibrium. Thealogical time, however, has its own pace and few Goddess feminists are pre-dicting the immediate demise of patriarchy. Rather, as patriarchy be-comes ever more ethically and ecologically unsustainable, they foresee a period of accelerated decline.

Goddess feminists do not see patriarchy as only self-extinguishing. It is believed that the Goddess who is manifest in the organic flow of change is now actively pulsing in the collective Western consciousness for the first time in about fifteen hundred years. This signals the 'natural' end of 'The Dark Age of Monotheism' (Shepsut 1993: 6) and with it, the possible resolution of the spiritual and ecological crises of modern patri-archy. Like others, Paula Gunn Allen believes that 'this is the time of the end—the end of patriarchy, the end of the profane. It is the time of the Grandmother's return, and it is a great time indeed' (Allen in Caputi 1993: xviii).

The revived vocation of priestess is regarded as a sign of the end of patriarchal religion and the dominatory culture it sanctions. Both Caitlín Matthews and Naomi Ozaniec, for example, believe that we are on the threshold of a new Goddess religion and a new historical epoch. Matthews envisages the present period being remembered as 'a revo-lutionary time when the Goddess walked among us. What kind of myth will they tell about our time I wonder?' (1989: 7). According to Ozaniec, this is a liminal, transitional stage in the history of religion; a 'potent and potentially dangerous time' requiring the mediation of a female priestess-hood (1993: 300). This is a priestesshood which, according to Asia Shepsut, is about to be born: 'The long atrophied gifts of the priestess are on the brink of painful re-emergence' (1993: 5).

The present historical transition is not one in which human beings are the sole agents of consciousness. The consciousness of the Goddess/ nature and spiritual feminist women is one. On a flight to Seattle in 1980, Mary Daly flew past the Mount Saint Helens volcano which was belching white smoke prior to a subsequent eruption a few days later. Daly's reminiscence of this moment is a good illustration of the unity of feminist and natural historical agency. She writes,

> I felt a deep kinship between her need to explode and my own . . .
> Mount Saint Helens spoke to me of the Elemental Biophilic Powers of
> the Earth and of women, as distinguished from destructive man-made
> necrophilic nuclear, chemical, and political pseudo-powers. That volcano
> said to me: 'Come on! Explode with me! Our Time is coming' (Daly
> 1993: 242).

In thealogy, the liberation of transformatory female energies from the religious and political structures that control, exploit and suppress them is considered central to the planetary future. In ways reminiscent of the nineteenth-century evangelical feminists who had absolute faith in women's moral and spiritual power to purify and redeem fallen humanity (see Hopkins 1899), spiritual feminists take the essentialist position that authentic, namely post-patriarchal, femaleness is salvific in itself. Charlene Spretnak speaks for all spiritual feminists when she claims that the true female mind, thinking in and through the body (that is, female embodied consciousness) will save the world from patriarchal annihilation and bring a new and just socio-ecological patterning to birth (1982: 565-73). Most spiritual feminists have real and realizable expectations for a post-patriarchal world and would support that envisaged in literary form in Starhawk's 1993 novel *The Fifth Sacred Thing*. Here the San Francisco Bay area of California is transposed into the mid-twenty-first century as an egalitarian, ecologically sustainable, cooperative, radically democratic, non-heterosexist, non-ageist, religiously plural and ethnically mixed community. Starhawk's utopia is in no way a matriarchal society where women rule over men; neither sex is materially or politically privileged over the other. Contrary to a common misconception about Goddess feminism, it does not look towards a matriarchal (as in female-dominant) future any more than it looks back to a matriarchal past.

The Purposes of Spiritual Feminist Historiography

An important purpose of spiritual feminist reconstructions of the ancient past is that of showing the peacefulness, and therefore the present desirability of Goddess-worshipping cultures. According to D.J. Conway, 'early matriarchal cities were not built on high, steep places; there were no enormous stone walls or hill forts'. For example, in Çatal Hüyük (a Neolithic settlement in southern Turkey excavated by James Mellaart in the early 1960s), 'there is absolutely no evidence of warfare for over 1,500 years' (Conway 1994: 14). Through their discussions of this and other such sites, spiritual feminists offer a historical precedent for global, ecological peacefulness and fund their belief that aggression is neither inevitable or natural to human existence, despite capitalist ideologies of competition for resources and survival suggesting that it is.

The apparently pacific nature of matrifocal religion and culture leads us to what is perhaps the most significant purpose of thealogical historiography, namely, to give evidence that patriarchy is not natural but historical. Patriarchy has justified its imposition of oppressive gender roles by claiming that they are ordained by God.[4] To transgress these roles is to transgress the law of God and the law of nature as God created it. Patriarchal philosophy and theology insists that men reason, moralize, legislate and theologize on behalf of women because women are, by virtue of their biological processes, rationally, morally and physiologically inferior and unreliable, and therefore innately prone to reduce the established order to chaos. Under patriarchy, the subordination of women is the prerequisite of social/cosmic order, but patterns of domination and subordination extend beyond that of women to (subject) men themselves. Although radical feminism regards the subordination of women to men as the type of all other subordinations, the ordered patriarchal hierarchy requires that the whole of creation—plants, animals, children, women, men and finally Christ are subordinate to the Fatherhood of God. Given that subject men also suffer under patriarchal systems, many spiritual feminists believe that their historiography is not undertaken on behalf of women alone, but might, in facilitating a return to the practices it uncovers, 'bring men back to themselves, as [the goddess] Isis resurrected [the god] Osiris' (Shepsut 1993: 3).

Like all feminists, spiritual feminists refuse to accept that patriarchy is the socio-political manifestation of the God-given—or even merely biological—dominance of the male. While most feminists do not speculate on the temporal origins of sexual inequality, but seek to demonstrate that inequality exists and to find ways of overcoming it, spiritual feminists are more ambitious. They want to say that patriarchy (which damages their very being as women, not just their socio-economic opportunities) has a beginning, and if it has a beginning, it can also have an end.

Goddess women can appeal to no Bible or creed to justify their faith in a pre-patriarchal world of prelapsarian harmony or the vision of a renewed, reconciled, ecologically balanced post-patriarchal world. It is more archaeology than the interpretation of sacred texts which might

---

4.   New Testament examples of the ordained subordination of women to men, particularly to husbands, include 1 Cor. 11.3, 7, 9; Eph. 5.22-24; 1 Tim 2.11-14; 1 Pet. 3.1.

justify their vision. Spiritual feminists gather archaeological, and some-times textual, evidence to show that patriarchy has a history of between five and six thousand years, whereas Goddess worship—and therefore reverence for femaleness as such—has a history of at least twenty-seven thousand years. One of the jobs of spiritual feminist historiography is, then, to put patriarchy in perspective; to say that historically (and often in ancient artistic representations) the Goddess dwarfs the god. More-over, research into the beginnings of patriarchal religion is intended to show that patriarchal religion is essentially, rather than contingently, misogynistic. That is, 'within the very structure of the contemporary male religions are the laws and attitudes originally designed to annihilate the female religions, female sexual autonomy and matrilineal descent' (Stone 1976: 228).

Although Goddess feminism is an ecological religion, spiritual femi-nists like Merlin Stone, Marija Gimbutas, Christine Downing, Asphodel Long and many others are concerned that the ancient Great Goddess is not identified exclusively with nature. The Goddess created and regu-lated civilization as well as life, and her ancient role as wise judge and measurer is researched and invoked as a way of breaking the patriarchal stereotype of women and goddesses as being ahistorical (promulgated through religious dogma and scholarship); of having purely reproductive functions. Goddess religion was and is inseparable from the cyclic pro-cesses of *both* nature and the history of civilizations and, ideally, these processes are in harmony with one another. Goddess religion is, there-fore, held to be not only a religion of nature but a natural religion. Goddess religion is, in this view, a religion that, if not strictly innate to human beings, is one which belongs to the very character of nature herself (because the Goddess *is* nature, though she is also more than the sum of nature's parts). Patriarchal, Abrahamic religion, by contrast, situ-ates itself in a transcendent (non) relation to nature, permitting the eco-nomic and social systems it sanctions to thrive upon the conquest and appropriation of natural/female products.

Spiritual feminism's sacred history also has an important part to play in bringing thealogy's political analysis out of the realm of theoretical abstraction and into the realm of experience. While modern Western patriarchy's religious indifference to nature and its technological ex-ploitation of natural resources have made it materially powerful, thealo-gians can show that such power is not as securely founded as it seems. First, spiritual feminism can make the ecological point that all living things, including elite human beings, are dependent on their natural environment. The climate and the condition of the earth, air and water must be such as to support life, and modern patriarchy is putting the planet under such pressure that it can no longer be guaranteed to continue to support any life. Patriarchal pressure on all living systems might be moving history towards a phase in which nature/the Goddess will no longer be able to support history and will, in order to save herself, bring that history to an end. Secondly, spiritual feminist history and archaeology can demonstrate that the power of nature/the Goddess is an older, stronger and different power to that of patriarchy; natural and cultural systems reverencing the female life principle will survive and outlive the male principle of domination because the latter is not only a historical aberration, it is also inherently (self-) destructive. This, then, is the locus of hope and faith in radical feminist religion and constitutes perhaps the deepest purpose of its historiography.

Spiritual Feminist Historiography

Around the same time as Gerder Lerner and Joan Kelly-Gadol were producing groundbreaking feminist arguments and methods for redefining history and for restoring women to history,[5] Goddess feminists like Marija Gimbutas, Riane Eisler and Merlin Stone were developing their own, parallel, criticism of the androcentric values, assumptions and methods of patriarchal or 'mainstream' archaeological, biblical and historical scholarship. (Marija Gimbutas, who died in 1994, was perhaps the best-known of these feminist scholars and the first to have articulated a feminist theory or reading of Neolithic culture [Marler 1996: 37-47].)

Feminist historians have pointed out that traditional historiography has had very limited, elitist, masculinist criteria for what *counts* as being of significant historical interest. Supporting their arguments, spiritual feminists have also questioned the religious and historical criteria for what counts in the past and present as good or true religion. In the early 1980s Charlene Spretnak observed that most theologians tend to assume that only religions with holy scriptures are legitimate religions and legitimate objects of research. Her response to this logocentric assumption was to say of Goddess religion, 'We are older, much older, than books' (1982: 5).

5.   Lerner (1979; Kelly-Gadol: [1983] 1976.) See also *Woman of Power* 16 (1990) dedicated to the theme of 'Re-Visioning History'.

Because the matrifocal period of Western Goddess religion is a pre-literate one, spiritual feminist reconstructions are dependent on a variety of sources other than purely textual ones and require a variety of inter-pretative methods. Goddess feminists must reinterpret ancient artifacts and sites, and reread the classical mythology (which debased the female divinities of the older mythology which had informed it [Daly 1991: 43-105]).[6] They must also reinterpret biblical scholarship's reading of ancient Near Eastern religion and archaeological accounts of ancient religion all over the world. So too, contemporary popular religious devo-tion in the less developed European cultures can also hold clues to, or memories of, older Western matrifocal belief (Birnbaum 1993). As they read, spiritual feminists must sieve out the patriarchal prejudices against matrifocal religion which have produced derogatory accounts of goddess worship, and sieve opinion from argument. They must notice the rever-sals, gaps and silences in academic studies of the history of women's religious and political roles and statuses. As non-feminist studies rarely focus on women or treat them as the subjects of their own experience, they must supplement fleeting references to women or the Goddess that can yield clues to matrifocal religion and culture and produce a kind of knowledge-by-default. In effect, then, almost any patriarchal religious rite, symbol, myth or text can be read so as to offer clues or traces of the matrifocal religion it might have supplanted (see Walker 1983).

This is arduous work. The spiritual feminist conviction that Goddess worship was never destroyed but persisted in countercultural or adulter-ated forms informs its historiographical methods (and also renders them extremely problematic to those who claim that they are not methods but the vehicles of speculation). De-Anna Alba, like all other Goddess feminists, observes that patriarchal domination has,

> made it more and more difficult to trace the thread of the Goddess run-ning throughout the web of the world and Western culture in particular. Although the thread has become twisted, knotted and obscured at times, in my opinion it has never been broken. The Goddess lives on, even within the Judeo-Christian traditions (1993: 15).

The interpretation of the biblical historical tradition is particularly con-tested territory between spiritual feminists and other scholars. The He-brew Bible records Israel's attempt to assert and consolidate its own

6.   Daly writes, 'patriarchal myths contain *stolen* mythic power . . . We can cor-rectly perceive patriarchal myths as reversals and pale derivatives of more ancient, more translucent myth from gynocentric civilization' (Daly 1991: 47).

cultic identity and territorial presence by destroying the Pagan religions within its conquered territories; religions that proved all too attractive to the Israelites themselves. Not only were Pagan shrines destroyed by Israelite religious leaders, Goddess feminist scholars commonly believe that the biblical scribes did not have the word 'Goddess' in their vocabulary and referred to her as 'Elohim' in the masculine gender (Stone 1976: xviii). However, Jewish feminists both within and outside the Goddess movement are rightly cautious of potentially anti-Semitic accusations of 'Goddess murder' against the Jews. As both Christ and Plaskow have done, Annette Daum points out that Judaism cannot be held solely responsible for the destruction of the matrifocal system; destruction of Goddess worship had begun long before the appearance of the Hebrews and was to continue until the fifth century CE under the Christians (Daum 1989: 305).

In any case, hostility to Paganism has not been confined to Jewish prophets, reformers and scholars. It has been in the theological interests of Christian as well as Jewish biblical scholars to discredit Israel's indigenous Pagan religions as orgiastic fertility cults presided over by 'temple prostitutes' (rather than priestesses), as lacking a concept of transcendence and being without ethical or legal codes (Ochshorn 1981: 127-29). (This despite the evidence in Joshua 9-11, for example, that the Israelites perpetrated unjustifiable atrocities on the Canaanites [Stone 1976: xix].) Within a culture informed by this monotheistic, patriarchal tradition, archaeologists are, not surprisingly, inclined to interpret ancient female figurines as fertility fetishes, erotic art or even as depictions of men rather than women (Conway 1994: 12). And when goddesses feature in the school curriculum many children assume that certain powerful ancient deities are male because the teachers, themselves schooled in androcentric scholarship, are not aware that such deities are female or take predominantly female forms (see Stone 1976: 9).[7]

Spiritual feminists are not suggesting that Goddess religion is the victim of an academic conspiracy. The silencing or denigration of prepatriarchal traditions is, rather, the product of 'a pervasive cultural attitude' which ensures that whatever religious practices have preceded or have not been taken into the sphere of Judaeo-Christian revelation are sub-religious or of negligible value (Spretnak 1982: 6). Moreover, Judaeo-Christian monotheism is almost compelled to make the *a priori*

---

7.   Stone asks, 'Was it merely coincidence that during all those years of Sunday School I never learned that Ashtoreth was female?' (1976: 9).

judgment that ancient Paganism was magical or sub-religious, for to claim otherwise would be to undermine its own claim to special revelation and to have established an ethically superior social order in God's name. In short, patriarchal scholarship operates within a context of much older, given 'authoritative' interpretations of the evidence for Goddess religion and, on religious and sexist assumptions, discounts the matrifocal meanings of the evidence from the outset. For spiritual feminists, as for the 'mainstream' academy, much more is at stake, then, in debates over ancient Goddess religion than winning or losing scholarly ground.

It must be admitted that spiritual feminist historiography has not had a great deal of direct impact upon the archaeological study of the ancient Near East or the textual study of the Hebrew Bible (Hackett 1989: 65). However, the spiritual feminist case has benefited from a number of archaeological finds over the last fifty years which seem to indicate the widespread presence of goddess worship in the ancient Near East (Eller 1993: 152). Even more readily assimilable to the spiritual feminist project are works by nineteenth and early twentieth-century anthropologists, folklorists and cultural historians, which used mythological texts and observation of contemporary 'primitive' practices, to argue (without feminist motives) that goddesses were originally pre-eminent over gods. In particular, mid-nineteenth-century social scientists and scholars of religion, seeking for the origins of religion and of human social institutions, were deeply influenced by J.J. Bachofen (1815–87) who argued that the first human societies were universally matriarchal and goddess-worshipping before they were conquered and replaced by patriarchy. Although this view did not go uncontested it was widely supported by diverse and influential theorists such Marx, Engels, Freud and Sir James Frazer, and was given a Jungian twist by Erich Neumann in 1955.

This type of 'matriarchal' theory has attracted spiritual feminist attention through the work of Marija Gimbutas, Pat Monaghan, Barbara Walker, Merlin Stone, Starhawk and others, though their use of such material has been regarded by the contemporary academic establishment as signalling the revival of an outdated, discredited theory that was marginal even at the time. However, spiritual feminists are certainly aware that there is a powerful patriarchal bias in nineteenth-century matriarchal theory and would want to make a clear distinction between patriarchal theories of matriarchy and their own contemporary theorizing of a woman-centred past (Göttner-Abendroth 1991: 223-24). In fact, Marija Gimbutas's research into the matrifocal, egalitarian and peaceful cultures she claims existed in Europe before the invasions of war-like Indo-European (patriarchal) tribes has been of greater and more immediate support to thealogians than has nineteenth-century matriarchalist theory (see Gimbutas 1974).

Despite its somewhat abstruse theoretical connections, spiritual feminist historiography is intended to be accessible to all women, not just scholars. (Semi-popular books like Riane Eisler's *The Chalice and the Blade: Our History, Our Future* sold about 206,000 copies within five years of its publication.) Spiritual feminist history cannot be reserved for academic specialists as, for thealogians, it has a redemptory function: that of helping to rebuild a derelict Goddess culture and, by doing so, to change the consciousness of those women who read their texts and believe their claims to be true. To have done its work properly, this narrative will have profoundly raised women's self-esteem by giving them a different sense of who and what they are and were.

In other words, Goddess feminist historiography has an ontological dimension. Merlin Stone, the author of perhaps the best-known work of spiritual feminist history, *When God Was a Woman*, began her study with the words, 'In the beginning, people prayed to the Creatress of Life, the Mistress of Heaven. At the very dawn of religion, God was a woman. Do you remember?' (1976: 1). These were some of the opening lines of a liberative, psychotherapeutic drama. In this drama contemporary women are both spectators and participants in the re-presentation of ancient women's spiritual and political power. There is no essential distinction made between women of the past and the present. Certainly, spiritual feminism does not want to say that the conditions of life and consciousness are or should be the same for ancient and modern women. But there is a real sense that nature stands outside historical time and that women's embodiment of the Goddess is an embodiment of her timeless generative energies. This thealogy of embodiment correspondingly produces a trans-historical consciousness to which the passage of patriarchal time is irrelevant. Time is, in thealogy, an essentially biological phenomenon, marked by the phases of the moon, the tides and the menstrual cycle. Women are not therefore divided from the past by the processes of historical change. Women 'recognise' their commonality with women and divinities from different cultures and periods, not by ahistorical claims that their lives are in some sense the same, but by the cyclic continuity of female embodiment across time.

Given the multi-dimensional nature of spiritual feminist historiography, it might be expected that spiritual feminists like the art historian and archaeologist, Asia Shepsut, are happy for spiritual feminist historical research to be conducted and mediated to other women by means other than scholarship alone. Shepsut's book, *Journey of the Priestess*, is given two subtitles, one academic and the other religious: *The Priestess Traditions of the Ancient World* and *A Journey of Spiritual Awakening and Empowerment*. Shepsut's inspiration for the book was a private religious experience:

> About a year ago I was lying on my sofa one evening and looking up at a Persian metalwork light globe, illuminated into a fretwork of dark against light, I felt the presence of a circle of women in the room around me. All I could discern was their comfortable bulk, and that they wore white scarves around their heads (Shepsut 1993: 3).

Shepsut tells us that this circle of women who 'visited' her was 'the present-day collective soul of those who wish again to wield true spiritual power in a world that needs it more than ever before' (1993: 10). Not only are some spiritual feminist historians practising a form of mediumship, they also derive historical knowledge and insight from ancient divinatory practices such as dreamwork, crystals and astrology which were themselves once practised by ancient priestesses and wise women (see Shepsut 1993: 11).

History is, therefore, accessible to feminist consciousness irrespective of whether it is accessible through texts, artifacts and archaeological sites. Asia Shepsut 'took the decision to walk back, psychologically, over the Bridge of Monotheism, which spans what turns out to be only a narrow divide between our modern world and the old'. Crossing these historical boundaries was a psychological and physical event. She travelled to ancient Goddess sites and monuments whose atmosphere 'sang in the ears at high frequency, electrifying the soul as it reconnected with far memory' (1993: 9). These sites mediated history/power to her directly.

In one recent issue of *Goddessing Regenerated* there were advertisements for Goddess tours or pilgrimages to a number of different countries: Hawaii, Turkey, Greece, Crete, Malta and the British Isles. To Goddess feminists, the ancient sites of the Goddess are not merely providing archaeological evidence for Goddess worship. As Carol Christ memorably demonstrates in her book *Odyssey With the Goddess*, leading a Goddess pilgrimage in Crete assumes (as any pilgrimage does) that these sites are sacred places in which the Goddess is still very much an object of experience. Carol Christ's 'Goddess Pilgrimage Tours' are advertised with the words, 'Feel Her [the Goddess's] power in holy mountains and sacred caves . . . transform the way you feel about women, yourself (advert in *Woman of Power* 1995: 84).

So too, the feminist shaman Vicki Noble runs an organisation called 'Sacred Journeys for Women', where she and Jennifer Berezan combine chanting, archaeology, rituals and shamanic practices to mediate the site's Goddess-energy to the feminist pilgrims. In an interview Noble clearly perceives her feminist, utopian vision as partially realized in the act of pilgrimage itself:

> I long for a return to the ways of the ancient Goddess-worshipping communities where women and children lived together and spent their days in activities that did not separate them from one another. I dream of those cultures where women governed themselves and their children with no antagonism from men. Every tour I lead to Greece or Malta or Ireland to visit ancient temples and stone circles is, for me, a reenactment of what it might be like to live our lives from matristic principles (Noble 1990: 71).

Thealogians have a marked distrust of the linear. What they understand to be the organic, cyclic, spiralling complexity of living, growing systems is quite different to the traditional biblical view of salvation history as a series of revelations which cuts sharply through nature, running in a straight line from creation to its eschatological *telos*. Spiritual feminism insists that reality is 'curved'; the Goddess generates the possibilities or ingredients of history by churning, spinning and stirring. The gestation of new historical possibilities takes place both metaphorically and actually in the cauldron-like womb of the Goddess.

This chaotic element of thealogy also characterizes its historiography. The Goddess is not, on the whole, conceived as an interventionist deity. World history runs its course without the Goddess 'stepping in' to avert disaster, even a disaster as great as the triumph of patriarchy and its modern assault upon nature—her body. Although Goddess feminists seem increasingly prepared to talk of their personal experiences of revelations of the Goddess as a guiding presence in their lives, spiritual feminism is usually reluctant to posit a Goddess who makes particular, world-historical, saving interventions. Most thealogy is hostile to the notion of one transcendent, controlling divine will and intelligence making decisions on behalf of everything else in the cosmos. The Goddess simply cannot be abstracted from nature or the cosmos to that degree; the pattern of the future is as undetermined as are complex living systems themselves.

Thealogy is most often a variety of Paganism and Pagan religions are typically circular: their purpose is to derive spiritual energy from living in rhythm with the turn of the seasons. Thealogy, like Paganism as a whole, does not subscribe to transcendental religions' redemptive narratives that promise a spiritual release from material finitude and change.

For this reason, some might argue that where Goddess feminism becomes a Pagan religion, it becomes too much a part of a cyclic (repetitive) and indeterminate reality to effect the historical liberation of women and nature from patriarchy which feminism has always sought. But this would be an oversimplification. If thealogy was entirely non-linear it would be difficult to retain any of its political purposiveness; its sense of time passing from matrifocal freedom to patriarchal captivity and on into the possibility of post-patriarchal freedom. In fact, there is no necessary contradiction in Goddess feminism's understanding of time as both linear and curved. Thealogy can, after all, describe linear, historical end-times, crises of political transition, and the rise and falls of civilizations as occurring on the turn of one cycle within a larger, continuous natural cycle of the death and rebirth of worlds.

Goddess women believe that Women/the Goddess once were, and can be again, cultural agents whose historical activity is grounded in the very activity of the cosmos itself. Moreover, the ancient goddesses reclaimed by thealogy are not merely goddesses of animal and human procreation. They could be 'fertility' goddesses in a far wider sense, namely goddesses of 'the cosmic principle of life, death and renewal' (Christ 1987: 167). As Merlin Stone points out,

> The Celtic Cerridwen was the Goddess of Intelligence and Knowledge in the pre-Christian legends of Ireland ... the Greek Demeter and the Egyptian Isis were both invoked as law-givers and sage dispensers of righteous wisdom, counsel and justice. The Egyptian Goddess Maat represented the very order, rhythm and truth of the Universe . . . while the archaeological records of the city of Nimrud, where Ishtar was worshipped, revealed that women served as judges and magistrates in the courts of law (Stone 1976: 4).

In sum, although spiritual feminists tend to write their history in accessible and abbreviated forms, their history is, *as historiography*, a complex web of political, archaeological and mythological criticism and reconstruction. Thealogy is not simply a religious discourse on the cycles of nature; it is also profoundly historical in character, carrying within it a story of the liberation of nature and civilization from patriarchy in chronological time. This is a dramatic story of primal happiness, loss, destruction and now, as we approach the millennium, the choice between life or death—between either liberative/ecological or capitalist/ militarist forms of social organisation.

Liberal Feminist Objections to Thealogical History

There is probably no more contentious subject for the feminist community than that of the religio-political character of prehistory. Of the contemporary feminist community, it is really only spiritual feminists who are persuaded of the historicity of a universal, matrifocal, pre-patri-archal culture. Feminist academics outside the Goddess movement generally argue that spiritual feminist historiography has simply jettisoned the normal academic endeavour of at least *trying* to assess and balance evidence in a rigorous, objective and disinterested manner. It is argued that spiritual feminist historiography is more thealogical and political than it is strictly historical in character; that, in less charitable words, much of it is simply wishful thinking.[8]

The feminist anthropologist Sally Binford has likened what she calls 'the myth of Former Matriarchal Greatness and the Overthrow of the Mother Goddess' to the myths of Adam and Eve and Pandora, and to Freud's account of penis envy. Comparing spiritual feminists' adherence to the 'matriarchal myth' with that of fundamentalists who are indifferent to scientific evidence for biological evolution, Binford writes, 'The tenacity with which many women cling to this belief is enormous. As an anthropologist, I am fascinated and can explain it only as a religious phenomenon' (1982: 542-43).

The Christian feminist Rosemary Ruether is also well known for her objections to spiritual feminist historiography. She argues that evidence for ancient goddess worship is not evidence for *feminist* religion, and the worship of goddesses did not (and, in the contemporary era, still does not) necessarily entail the high social status of women.[9] As Jo Ann

8. See the debate between Binford, Spretnak and Stone in Spretnak 1982: 541-61.
9. Reuther 1980: 843. In response, Carol Christ argues that Ruether has not considered evidence of the earlier Goddess cultures and images dating from the Neolithic period, but has focused instead on evidence from 3500 BCE and later, by

Hackett puts the point, 'If you want to celebrate ancient female divine power, do it, but first find out what it was' (1989: 76). Liberal feminist scholars tend to agree with 'mainstream' anthropologists and historians of religion who argue that, while goddess worship evidently played a prominent role in the religious life of the Upper Paleolithic era, we cannot deduce an early matriarchy of the sort described by Goddess feminists from the archaeological evidence alone. The meaning of excavated goddess figurines should not be abstracted from that of masculine and animal images of the period which might provide a more comprehensive picture of gender and early religion. More generally, reformist feminists seek a liberated future through legal and religious reform, not through archaeological excavation and the revival of politically and theoretically dubious nineteenth-century matriarchalist theories.

While these reformist arguments can be persuasive, for some spiritual feminists the *idea* or myth of a matrifocal age is as important (or more so) than its reality. Even if there never were matristic societies, that does not mean that there never could be, or that the idea could not bring such imaginings into the conditions of possibility. Thus Starhawk: 'whether or not there was a religion of the Great Goddess in prehistoric times, there is one today. Whether or not women ever ruled in matriarchies, women are taking power today' (1982a: 415). So where sacred history has the effect of raising consciousness of personal/political power, it matters little whether it is history or mythology. The narration of sacred history can have real effects: 'In this sense a remembered fact and an invented fantasy have identical psychological value' (Goldenberg 1979: 89).

Perhaps prehistory is so distant from the present as to be almost indistinguishable from the sacred time in which myths are replayed. Moreover, it is arguable that all historiography has, in any case, imaginative, narrative and even mythographical elements. Postmodern historians have pointed out that all historiography is substantially determined by the gender, class, national and racial, religious and intellectual interests of the historian, and that no historical research is conducted in an

which time Goddess worship may indeed reflect patriarchal culture (1987: 64). Ruether does, however, affirm the value of contemporary reconstructions of ancient images of the Goddess to religious feminists. For example, Ruether finds that the written evidence of the Goddess from between 2800 and 1200 BCE is free from any gendered division of divine labour and as such, 'provides the most striking alternative to the symbolic world generated by male monotheism' (1983: 52).

entirely neutral or objective manner. There is no unmediated access to the past and thealogy filters through its own spiritual/political lens what (mainly) patriarchal scholarship can tell us about Goddess religion's past. This is not to say that historiography can be an imaginative free-for-all, but that in the case of ancient or pre-literate religious history, it is especially difficult to keep the religious and political purposes of reconstruction from determining the nature of the reconstruction itself. Where sources are few and difficult to interpret, it is not easy to see where reconstruction turns into imaginative re-invention.

However, if spiritual feminist historiography is closer to mythopoesis than it usually claims to be, then its feminist critics might justly prefer that it renounce its aggravating claim to historical scholarship. Furthermore, to treat patriarchy as a temporary historical aberration may mislead feminists into failing to take patriarchal power sufficiently seriously and failing to acknowledge women's complicity with those patriarchal systems which have conferred a degree of power or material benefit upon them.

In conclusion, over the course of this chapter I have tried to show that while the *idea* of a matrifocal past can take thealogy a long way, most spiritual feminists make a considerable emotional and scholarly investment in its historicity. Were their claim of an original, global gynocentric culture shown conclusively to be true, the case for Goddess religion would be substantially advanced in so far as patriarchal religion and culture could be shown to be neither historically inevitable nor intrinsic to the natural or created order.

However, the fate of spiritual feminism does not hang upon the verdict of the historical or religious academy. As Daphne Hampson has noted, most 'Goddess religion is thoroughly syncretistic, women weaving together ancient symbols and newly created myths' (1990: 111). Perhaps the conflation of these ancient images and symbols with new myths, irrespective of their historical context, could spark daring new religio-political projects that would be the more visionary for their lack of a knowable historical precedent.

Chapter Four

Thealogy and Ethics

The Goddess contains within Herself all energies and is the centre from where they emanate. She can live with paradoxes and mystery and Her message to us is: 'As I dying live, so you dying will live again.' In the natural world, light and dark are interwoven without contradiction and disharmony (Sjöö 1992: 126).

Since the early 1980s feminist ethics has developed as an academic discipline in response to moral philosophy's tradition of androcentric, disembodied and often absolutist ethical deliberations. Although feminist ethics is a diverse terrain, it is unified by its proposal that ethics be practised in a contextual or situated and egalitarian manner. Following the publication of Carol Gilligan's enormously influential *In a Different Voice: Psychological Theory and Women's Development* (1982) feminist ethicists commonly argue that all ethicists should learn from the relational, caring and practical ways in which women are culturally or biologically attuned to make moral choices.

Feminist ethical discourse has also arisen in protest against patriarchal religious ethics' and philosophy's defamation of women as congenitally less capable of rational thought than men and, therefore, less morally reliable. In cataloguing the history of religious and philosophical misogyny, religious feminism has analysed the religio-political textual and legal forms through which patriarchy has denied women's full humanity, ascribing to them instead a tendency to blind emotion and the temptation and distraction of men from their higher will and duty. Under the most conservative forms of patriarchy, the view that women are rationally and morally inferior to men, to this day, justifies keeping women under the discipline of fathers, husbands, brothers and clergy, and excludes women from the given religion's most sacred spaces and statuses, and from the formulation and the interpretation of religious legislation and sacred texts.

Religious feminism has, then, supplied the background which helps us to understand why and how women have been denied full ethical agency. Religious feminism has also made a further contribution to feminist ethics, though it is not one that always figures prominently in the academic literature of secular feminist ethics. That is, most religious feminism, including Goddess feminism, is premised on the principle of ecological and spiritual interconnection. The journal *Woman of Power* states its relational philosophy on the front page of its journal and it is one with which few religious feminists would quarrel:

> Our power as women arises from our understanding of interconnectedness; with all people, all forms of life, the earth, and the cycles and seasons of nature and our lives. Through this understanding we commit ourselves to the transformations necessary for the renewal of our selves and our planet (1995: 1).

The Basis of Thealogical Ethics

The view that women and nature have been profoundly harmed by patriarchal religion's drive towards the transcendence and subjugation of female sexuality and nature is founded in thealogy's contrary claim that the being and processes of the divine are best imaged as female in character and that the divine is immanent in nature and within the web of relationships nature sustains. Whereas in classical theism a transcendent divinity issues commands and confers value from outside a natural world that has little or no intrinsic value *as* natural, in Goddess religion all living things already participate in the value of the Goddess who is present in the world as the dynamic or loving matrix of life itself. This means that all living things *matter* and no person need aspire to the super-natural perfection of a transcendent deity unlimited by the conditions of finitude. When the divine is immanent in all things, each agent must honour their own divinity and that of their natural environment, of which they are wholly a part.

Although it is arguable that Goddess religion's preoccupation with nature and its refusal to dualize good and evil has deprived it of an adequate concept of justice, Carol Christ would deny that this is the case. This is because,

> In Goddess religion, the source of morality is the deep feeling of connection to all people and to all beings in the web of life. We act morally when we live in conscious and responsible awareness of the intrinsic value

of each being with whom we share life on earth. When we do so, we
embody the love that is the ground of all being [that is, the Goddess]
(1997: 156).

If one accepts Christ's, highly contentious, first premise that nature is
'intelligent and loving', then one might also accept that loving, relational moral behaviour can be, as she claims, rooted in nature, obviating
any need for transcendental laws of love and justice. Citing Simone de
Beauvoir, Christ points out that a love and respect for life—which she
finds above all in Goddess religion—is the precondition of ethical goodness. Without loving life and the living for their own sake, no abstract,
transcendent command to love will be of any avail, especially not one
that operates within an ethos of domination (1997: 156-57).

Refusing the patriarchal ethos of domination, Christ advances, not an
exhaustive set of thealogical ethical precepts, but nine 'touchstones'
which can be adapted to a given context. These are:

Nurture life.
Walk in love and beauty.
Trust the knowledge that comes through the body.
Speak the truth about conflict, pain and suffering.
Take only what you need.
Think about the consequences of your actions for seven generations
Approach the taking of life with great restraint.
Practice great generosity.
Repair the web (1997: 166-67).

Clearly, these touchstones would not be peculiar to Goddess feminists
and do not presuppose a concept, experience or affirmation of the Goddess. This wise counsel would also be familiar and acceptable to all
Pagans and to those on the greener wings of Christianity and Judaism.

Christ has tried to translate the 'mythos' of Goddess religion into an
'ethos'. So too, Goddess feminists would want to base their ethos upon
the primary historical act of the restoration of the Goddess in Western
culture. This act of restoration would itself be a paradigmatically ethical
act of justice-seeking and restitution and one which, if successful, would
restore the possibility of justice and dignity to women and all silenced,
oppressed peoples. For if the erasure of the Goddess's presence and
power was a primary act of violence, environmental destruction and oppression, her restoration and that of those peaceful, wise, just matrifocal
values which attended and still attend her (feminist) celebration will
restore peace, wisdom and justice to society and ecological balance to
the ecosphere.

Starhawk has been Goddess feminism's most influential ethicist. Although the web-like, unowned process of thealogical discourse I referred to in the introduction to this book means that her ethic is not claimed to be her invention and nor does it have legislative authority, Starhawk's ethical precepts have, nonetheless, met with widespread spiritual feminist approval. The ethic she proposes usefully exemplifies not only feminist Wiccans' but most spiritual feminists' understanding of the ethical process and what it means for a thealogian to think and act ethically.

Starhawk argues that there is no metaphysical good outside the flourishing of life. In thealogy a moral agent acts in accordance with the natural laws that secure the ecological harmony and balance that underpins the entirety of planetary well-being. For human beings, the well-being of a strong, unbroken planetary web offers the spiritual/emotional and material well-being for the greatest number of living things, human or otherwise. The consequences of wrong-doing are, then, as Starhawk puts it, 'inherent in the structure of the world'. If we pollute the world we will inevitably suffer an increased incidence of miscarriages, birth defects and cancer: 'That is the way it works.' Starhawk writes: 'no external God, Goddess, angel or convoy of visitors from another planet' will establish justice on our behalf; '*We* must create justice and ecological and social balance' (1982a: 417, 421).

The necessity for divine justice in biblical religion assumes human and natural moral deficiency. But thealogy does not make this assumption. For despite the real historical suffering wrought by the coming of patriarchy, there is nothing inherently wrong with nature or with human beings. For Starhawk, in experiencing the Goddess, 'we can open new eyes and see that there is nothing to be saved from . . . There is only the Goddess, the Mother, the turning spiral that whirls us in and out of existence' (1982b: 56).

In thealogy, the fate of the cosmos is not bound up with that of human life. And the earth does not suffer the consequences of human wrong-doing as it does, say, in the biblical story of Noah and the Flood. Conversely, humans are not privileged with a status or place apart from nature. The Goddess is not only manifest in human consciousness, but in the whole living world. Thus Goddess religion's ethical imperative is to honour the Goddess through care and respect for the whole community of life, not just human life. In thealogy, the Goddess has none of the holiness of, say, the God of orthodox Judaism whose revelation must be kept apart from the profanity or impurity of disease and decay; on the contrary, the Goddess 'dances amid the concrete and the garbage embracing us all' (Javors 1990: 214).

However, the Goddess is not best celebrated or manifest in conditions of disempowerment. Poverty, discrimination and ecological degradation diminish her/our energy, making it necessary for spiritual feminists to work for political change. Contradicting those feminists who claim that thealogy is a bourgeois spiritual indulgence, Starhawk writes, 'we cannot fulfil ourselves in a world of starvation, pollution and hopelessness' (1982a: 417-19).

Starhawk's ethic unites personal, political and ecological action within one religious ethic. Moreover, by rooting thealogical ethics in the well-being of the whole environment, Starhawk avoids setting transcendent, acontextual moral principles over and against human health and happiness. For example, when traditional Catholics ban birth control in the name of transcendent sacred principles, she claims that they 'cause pain and suffering in pursuit of an unmanifest good'. Theirs is not a deliberate infliction of suffering but the pursuit of an abstract religious good which often causes suffering by default (poverty, the neglect of children and so forth). By contrast, the erotic or biophilic, contextual nature of thealogical ethics is a function of the Goddess's immanence in the world and her self-manifestation in human pleasures and needs (1982a: 416).

Such views have, not surprisingly, been countered or at least modified by other feminists. Goddess feminists are frequently criticized for presupposing in the cosmos a strict duality between 'good' female energies and 'bad' male energies; the one nurturant and the other destructive. Reformist feminism has usually taken the position that gender is socially produced; that there are no essential or biological moral characteristics peculiar to each sex. For reformists, virtue and vice are not determined by sex: men are not invariably aggressive and destructive and women are not invariably peace-loving and nurturing. For example, it is undeniable that some women's standards of living have benefitted from slavery and the misappropriation of land and property during and after genocide. Once given equal opportunities to participate fully in the political process, women are demonstrably as corruptible as men.

Janet McCrickard, for example, has accused Goddess women of a fundamentalist 're-writing of history as a dualistic battle between good (us) and evil (them)'. She claims that women assume for themselves all the 'feminine' qualities of the lunar principle: cooperation, magic and new life, in opposition to those of the fierce masculine solar principle: hier-archy, science and death (1991: 62-63). Although McCrickard's view is an oversimplification, it is not entirely wide of the mark. Barbara Walker, thealogy's foremost historian of religion, expresses a fairly typi-cal thealogical estimation of the moral standing of each sex, writing that,

> if women's religion had continued, today's world might be less troubled by violence and alienation. Gods, including Yahweh, tended to order their followers to make war; whereas the great mother Goddesses advo-cated peaceful evolution of civilised skills (Walker 1983: x).

When, in the terminology of Wilhelm Reich, spiritual feminists claim that men are 'on the neuron level wired for oppression' (Sjöö and Mor 1991: 18) or that they have an insatiable vampiric lust for female blood; that the 'he-male' is a 'bloodthirsty monster', or a 'Male Machine' (Daly 1985: 172-73), they do little to correct the impression that many God-dess feminist's distrust of men is not just politically but also ontologically grounded. Whether or not that is the case, there is no doubt that the central ethico-religious dynamic of spiritual feminism is its vision of the inherent nature of gynocentric culture as a biophilic one. This vision depends on faith that women will and, by and large, do, make better use of power than men.[1]

This chapter is intended to convey a sense of the subtlety and com-plexity of thealogical ethics. Two points, however, need to be borne in mind when considering thealogical ethics. First, thealogy is not, primar-ily, the province of academic theorists. It is still an experiential, (semi-) popular discourse, and spiritual feminists are far more likely to derive their ethics from their concepts of nature, biology, sexuality and mater-nal care than most feminist ethicists in the academy would be willing to do (see, e.g., Amberston 1991: 61). Most spiritual feminists, for example, believe that war is men's negative, but self-empowering, imitation of women's menstruation, and that male religion and war require the vio-lence of sacrificial blood-letting to compensate for their lack of magical, life-giving menstrual blood. Secondly, although it is particularly marked

---

1.   If women are now complicit in patriarchal oppression that is because they are, in Daly's view, 'token-torturers': women so morally and spiritually damaged by patriarchy that they avenge their suffering by visiting the same wounds on younger women as they themselves received at the hands of the female 'token-torturers' before them. Patriarchy, hiding behind women, exploits 'token-torturers' as instru-ments by which to divide women against one another—and so diffuse their power —making them easier to control (1991: 132, and esp. 163-65).

in some thealogy, the gendering of good and evil is not confined to thealogy alone but is characteristic of much of the radical or romantic feminist tradition which has tended to attribute inherent virtues to women *as* women and mothers. Other radical or romantic feminist ethicists like Nel Noddings and Sara Ruddick also emphasize maternal care and nurture as the heart of feminine moral agency (Noddings 1984; Ruddick 1990).

Ecofeminism and Reproductive Choice: Two Examples of Thealogical Ethics in Action

In 1980, after the Three Mile Island nuclear catastrophe, Ynestra King and other feminist activists organized a historic conference in Amherst, Massachusetts on 'Women and Life on Earth: Ecofeminism in the 1980s'. This conference, along with other ecofeminist conferences held at this time, were to forge the now central ecofeminist element of the women's movement, along with the publication of Susan Griffin's haunting, powerful book *Woman and Nature* in 1978 and Carolyn Merchant's more analytical *The Death of Nature* in 1980, the growth of the women's peace movement, and the increasing acceptance of evidence that women, human embryos, babies and children are first to suffer the impact of environmental degradation.

What unites ecofeminists is the belief that the patriarchal exploitation of the earth and of women are connected. A long history of anthropocentrism and androcentrism has rendered nature subordinate to human (predominantly male) needs and to the creation of human meaning. Furthermore, the patriarchal view that nature/women represent the lower, bodily qualities of the material world, and that the male soul or mind represents the higher, ordering qualities of culture and divinity has structured a dualism which permits men to subjugate nature/women for the sake of human and cosmic harmony. Ecofeminism argues that nature is not a mere resource and, more than that, it traces the roots of all oppression and exploitation to this pervasive dualism. Ecofeminism argues for nothing less than a paradigm shift which would dissolve such dualism and would entirely re-vision the relationship of humanity to all other forms of being.

There are, however, several different types of ecofeminism, and these are commonly classified under the headings of reformist, socialist and radical/spiritual feminist. To understand this last type of ecofeminism it needs to be set in a brief comparative context with the other types of ecofeminist analysis (cf. Merchant 1990: 100-102).

Liberal or reformist feminism seeks to protect the environment through legislative reform. Socialist ecofeminists argue that neither women nor nature should constitute a marketable resource and that only a socialist revolution could restructure the global economics that commodify nature. Radical or spiritual ecofeminism is commonly criticized by both liberal and socialist ecofeminists for indirectly reaffirming and perpetuating patriarchy's insistence on the naturalness of women and that of traditional women's culture: precisely the ideological space liberal feminism has wanted to redeem women from (see, e.g., Jaggar 1983: 18-22, 27-47). A great deal of such criticism has been levelled at radical or spiritual ecofeminism and it does not need lengthy repetition here. For the purposes of this study, it seems more important to try to elucidate the position itself as spiritual ecofeminist philosophy and activism are among the defining characteristics of the thealogical perspective.[2]

The spiritual ecofeminist perspective shares elements of the liberal and socialist ecofeminist perspectives, but for spiritual ecofeminism the earth and women's bodies (which, in effect, become one and the same) have intrinsic sacred value as 'female' entities. Nature becomes conscious and in some ways personal as the power of the Goddess—a power which will prove infinitely greater than the religious and modern scientific methods used to subdue her. Goddess women believe that a unified, unstoppable, female/natural/divine power is realized through ritual and ritualised direct action and of women coming to experience ownership over their own biological process and of the cosmic dimensions of that generative process.

At variance with most forms of traditional Christianity, Goddess feminism affirms not only the sacredness of life, but also the religious value of *being* alive and of the sensual, non-exploitative enjoyment of naturalness. As the feminist witch De-Anna Alba says of the world, 'We like it here. We enjoy incarnation on Earth and consider it sacred' (1993: 11). Therefore things considered morally wrong by Goddess feminists are not always considered morally wrong by patriarchal religionists (and vice versa).

---

2.   Helpful discussions of the spiritual ecofeminist dimension of Goddess feminism include, Spretnak (1990: 3-14); Starhawk (1990: 73-85); *idem* (1989: 174-85). A number of other articles in Plant's edited collection are also relevant.

This is particularly the case with regard to environmental ethics. Under certain conservative interpretations, the Bible permits or endorses human dominion over nature; nature is a resource which God has left entirely at our disposal. By contrast, the plunder of land and sea and the cruel rearing and slaughter of animals for human profit is considered absolutely wrong by spiritual feminists; not simply because it demonstrates greed and indifference to suffering, but because thealogical ethics are grounded in a spiritual perception of the unity of all living things in the Goddess.

For Goddess feminists, the exploitation of nature as a subjugated object is a religious crime as well as ecological folly. Claire Cranwell, for example, argues that vegans—who desist from eating dairy produce as well as meat—are above all rejecting the exploitation of female animals. Mother-animals are exploited for their reproductive yield and suffer separation from their young and other abuses precisely *as* female animals. Noting the connections between the patriarchal predation, abuse and derogation of human and non-human female animals, Cranwell argues that feminist veganism is a peace-loving way of life that is mindful of the worship of animals such as cows in gynocentric, pre-patriarchal societies and, more significantly, is 'critical for the well-being and survival of our Earth Mother'. Cranwell's Goddess feminist veganism is, in short, an opportunity to respect her animal and human 'earthling sisters' and at the same time to express her love for the Goddess (1997: 4-5).

Thealogy is, by its very nature, ecofeminist (though, of course, not all ecofeminists are Goddess feminists). What thealogy contributes to eco-feminism and to the women's movement as a whole is its contention that feminism cannot succeed on a purely intra-human, political basis. The naturalness of all reality; the denial that the sacred is *super*natural, demands that liberation be systemic throughout nature, not just confined to white Western women, as has so often been the case in the Women's Liberation Movement. Any liberative project that seeks less than the liberation and sacralization of land, seas, animals and plants, as well as of all subject human beings, will leave the social/natural ecology almost as out of balance as it was before.

The ontological continuity between women, nature and the Goddess entail that all three suffer as one from the desecration that is patriarchy's exploitation of the 'female' capacity to generate life. This view of patriarchy as definitively exploitative is more forcefully propounded in spiritual ecofeminism than in any other type of ecofeminism. Indeed, thealogical ethics as a whole is not fully comprehensible without first taking the measure of the thealogy of patriarchy. Patriarchy, in most thealogians' understanding (and notably Daly's), is a 'necrophilic', death-dealing system whose energy is derived from its three-stage colonization of female/natural bodies. First, patriarchy desacralizes femaleness; that is, it denies or strips away its sacred status thus placing its sacred powers of generation under the control, and at the disposal of, patriarchal religio-political authorities. Once rendered powerless, female bodies can be efficiently parasitized; their energies redirected to fuel the patriarchal project. Finally, parasitized women/nature are left politically and emo-tionally dis-spirited and in the dangerously weakened, wasted state we witness today as the effects of ecological and spiritual degradation become ever more visible and systemic in the greed, violence and alien-ation that characterizes so much contemporary culture.

For thealogy, all of life is held within (or is symbolically summarized by) the sensate body of the Goddess. Patriarchy gains God-like control over life to the extent that it can colonize women's/nature's bodies with impunity. In modernity, technology has permitted atrocities of coloniza-tion against the Goddess that early (Bronze Age) patriarchy had already set in train, but on a scale and with techniques it could not have dreamed of:

> She is dynamited, she is strip-mined, she is gassed and sprayed with chemicals. She is riddled with wells seeking oil, her blood, determined to seek out the last black drop. Her brain, which is the sea, is dumped full of poison. The air through which she breathes, becomes a thick toxic cloud . . . (Sjöö and Mor 1991: 412).

In thealogy, not only war, but pornography, rape, battering, genital and cosmetic mutilation and gynaecological abuse are some of the 'fallout' from the primary patriarchal violation of the body of the Goddess. Hence Goddess women's religious experience of the essential unity of all life in the Goddess, and their consciousness of assaults upon any living thing being assaults upon themselves, establishes a highly focused ethic. If the crimes done to one are done to all and, finally, felt by all, then the responsibility to protest and to heal is a collective one. The web-like unity of life in the Goddess magnifies the nature of crimes against living things to that of Goddess-murder or deicide. The suffering produced by patriarchal crimes against life reverberates, proliferates and disperses within the ecological whole. To that extent, thealogical ethics is characterized by a sense of urgency and anger that is now rarely found in other parts of the contemporary feminist movement. For example, the spiritual/emotional experience of the sacred unity of life in the Goddess can produce magico-political activists like The Clan of the Rowan Tree who—because they are sisters, mothers and daughters to one another and to the earth—are as much (or more) prepared to risk confrontations with the legal establishment in their struggle against injustice as any other group of feminists.

Thealogy's distinctive account of a Goddess woman as one who, in Daly's words, 'casts her lot, life, with the trees and the winds, the sands and the tides, the mountains and the moors' (1984: 3) *can* be politically escapist. It can also be defeatist where it implies that it is no longer worth feminists working for the transformation of human culture. But this shift into another ontological and existential mode can also have an unexpectedly political dimension. The 'Wild Women' described by Daly, Clarissa Pinkola Estés, Laurel King, Zsuszanna Budapest and others (see, e.g., Estés 1992; King 1993; Goldberg 1990) need not be those whose reintegration with the natural process entails their neglect of the political process. On the contrary, it can reconfigure the terms and methods of their political engagement. As I have argued elsewhere, (Raphael 1997b: 56-63, 65-68) when Goddess women return to their 'naturalness', that is, when their consciousness and values are no longer mediated by patriarchy, they will come truly and fiercely to life. This is because when a thealogian speaks of a woman recovering her naturalness she is indicating that a woman is recovering from patriarchy; taking possession of herself once more. Also, and more fundamentally, what is natural is of the Goddess and will share in her energies and powers— powers which have political ramifications as the very dynamics of all change, including emancipatory change.

The ethical implications of the thealogy of nature can also be traced through spiritual feminism's response to the question of the abortion of unwanted foetuses, and as thealogical 'pro-choice' arguments are also generally unfamiliar to those otherwise versed in the 'mainstream' debate between the 'pro-choice' and the 'pro-life' factions, it is to this issue that I now turn.

For Goddess feminists, women's right to abortion on demand is not only a political and economic necessity, but also a spiritual necessity. The Jungian psychologist Ginette Paris's book (whose title is off-puttingly translated as *The Sacrament of Abortion*) presents a Pagan feminist argument that abortion is a woman's *religious* choice. For Paris, abortion is both a sacrificial and, paradoxically, a nurturing act in which a pregnant woman gives responsible moral and spiritual consideration to a balance of interests: for the well-being of her self, the potential child, her other children, her economic situation and the ecological environment.

Paris argues that patriarchal religionists have held onto power by denying that 'a woman has the power to make a moral judgement that involves a choice of life or death. That power has been reserved for men' (1992: 25). Patriarchy defends its hold on the political and sacred power to ordain life by the argument that it is protecting the sanctity of life. But for religious and political legislation to *force* a woman to give birth is, for spiritual feminists, the true violation of the sanctity of life. Life is freely given by the Goddess and by women who choose to become mothers (Paris 1992: 62; Starhawk 1982a: 420). To honour the moral and spiritual nature of a woman's choice to abort, and to meet its attendant need for spiritual and physical healing, there is an urgent need for 'new rituals as well as laws to restore to abortion its sacred dimension, which is both terrible and necessary' (Paris 1992: 92-93).

Goddess feminism's view that women 'own' their own bodies—indeed, *are* their own bodies—and therefore have the right to full reproductive choice, is one that is shared with contemporary feminism as a whole. But, differently, the thealogical pro-choice stand emerges from a distinct understanding of patriarchy as a paradigmatically immoral state that (though globally diverse) is primarily dependent on a desecration and colonization of bodies that is sanctified by patriarchal religion. Under patriarchy a married woman can be reduced from an incarnation of Goddess power to a breeding machine; her uterus producing wealth in the form of children. Patriarchy then appropriates these children (particularly male children) by turning them against their mothers and 'soft' maternal values. Young adults are then deployed to perpetuate and augment patrilineally inherited and controlled property by giving birth to more children or by being traded as labourers or killers who will fight patriarchy's wars over natural resources and ideological supremacy. Whether by production or destruction, women's biological yield is used to yield more land and wealth for the patriarchal elite (Sjöö and Mor 1991: 359-65).

Under these conditions it is felt to be essential for women to recognize the political connection between biological reproduction and economic production. Women can only begin to reclaim political power when they can exercise full reproductive choice. For thealogy, this choice is underpinned by a female/maternal rather than a male/paternal concept of divinity, entailing that the best conditions for motherhood are central and immediate to the discussion.

Thealogy's spiralling rather than linear distinction between life and death reconfigures the terms and questions of the whole debate. Thealogy redefines the question of a foetus's 'right to life'. Goddess women refuse to accept obscure, philosophical/ideological patriarchal deliberations over the point at which a foetus's life has begun and cannot, therefore, be terminated and whether a foetus can be called a person before it has duties and responsibilities. Their argument is centred on an understanding of the woman as both autonomous individual and, at the same time, 'not a separate isolated *object*'. She belongs to 'a nexus of interwoven relationships' within the whole biological community (Starhawk 1982a: 418). Starhawk argues that 'Goddess religion recognizes that to value life as an untempered absolute is ridiculous'; no cell, virus or organism can multiply endlessly: 'life is interwoven in a dance of death, the limiting factor that sustains the possibility of new life' (1982a: 420).

Neither a woman's decision to abort, nor the foetus itself, exists in a social or ecological vacuum. As Monica Sjöö and Barbara Mor argue,

> Life does not begin. It is always here. Nature is alive from the beginning, and prodigal. Life does not emerge *from us*, we emerge *from it*. Pregnancy and childbirth are ritual passages of eternal life through the bodies of autonomous women.

If 'continuous waste and death occurs [sic] within a continuous sea of life', life cannot become the property of individuals suddenly at the moment of conception, but is a cycle beginning with the origins of the earth and of which all things are a part. Both the earth and the womb's power to bring forth new life is sacred and, like any sacred thing, cannot be owned as property. Nature is not only sacred, it is, according to Goddess women, intelligent or conscious. Accordingly, thealogy invites women to 'listen' to and trust the promptings of their own bodies: 'we must begin believing, or rebelieving, that the female being, of its own original nature, *knows* what it has to do, when it must be done, and why' (Sjöö and Mor 1991: 386-88).

In common with most other feminists, spiritual feminists make the practical point that to deny women freedom of reproductive choice has less to do with patriarchy's concern for the well-being of children than its will to control women's sexuality and reproductive yield. After all,

people with true concern for young lives would make their first priorities the establishment of world peace, the banning of nuclear and
chemical weapons, the control of pesticides and chemical emissions, and
the provision of free, safe and effective contraceptive methods and education, good child care facilities and safe play spaces—which, by and
large, those patriarchal religionists who forbid abortion do not.

It is not that spiritual feminists would take the decision to abort
lightly. Abortion is, for most women, a painful choice—all the possibilities that come with bringing a new person into the world are lost.
Under patriarchy, this pain is often distorted to one of guilt. Thealogy
refuses to make abortion more traumatic than it need be by making it
synonymous with infanticide. Undertaken with proper consciousness of
its meaning and with care and respect for the mother and the foetus, an
abortion is not a moral crime but part of a much larger natural/divine
process. For Zsuszanna Budapest,

> Abortion is the prerogative of the Dark Mother; she aborts us monthly; it
> is called menses. The shadow of motherhood is abortion, which is also
> our responsibility; making the choice of life and death are as much a part
> of the Goddess as her life-giving good nature (1989: 127).

Good, Evil and the Goddess

Rita Gross, a feminist scholar of religion, has suggested that the 'dominant emphasis' of thealogy is its 'contention that, minus patriarchy, the
world would be a utopia' (1986: 39). While she admits that patriarchy
imposes 'unnecessary' suffering on humanity, there is, she says, an 'irre-
ducible' kind of suffering peculiar to finite human life, 'that is simply
not patriarchy's fault'. Gross accepts that 'a feminist program for social
transformation would induce a revolution in the quality of life and that
this revolution would promote the best possible social arrangements'
(1986: 40-41). But she urges spiritual feminists to give up on feminism
as a total existential solution and on 'glib devotion' to the Goddess.
Feminists should instead foster real experiential understanding of the
Goddess as a 'symbol of the coincidence of opposites, imaged as Lady of
the Round, Mistress of Death and Birth'. Gross, who has long been
inspired by the fearsome Indian goddess, Kali, argues that Crone images
of the Goddess such as Kali can help women to develop feminist theo/
alogy's basic claim that finitude must be taken seriously (Gross 1986:
44). It is, after all, patriarchy's resistance to finitude that has denigrated

nature and femaleness, and, in its bid for immortality may, indeed, have led to the extinction of Goddess imagery in the West (1986: 43-45).

Gross is, I think, unfair to most thealogians.[3] In this study, I have argued that thealogy at its most persuasive argues in precisely the way she has suggested. I myself have not come across sentimental *feminist* thealogies which render the Goddess in the comforting image of patriarchal femininity, rather the opposite. While spiritual feminism's view of a post-patriarchal world is idealistic, it is not presented as the thealogical equivalent of heaven. Thealogy is not merely tolerant of existential ambiguity or paradox, but celebrates it as interwoven into the very life-giving character of the cosmos and therefore of the divine (Starhawk and Culpepper 1989: 105-109). Goddess feminists do not shy away from rage, death and destruction when it is grounded in the Goddess's preservation of ecological balance.

A Goddess feminist's actual ethical choices cannot be fully understood without placing them in a broader context of thealogical discourse on good and evil. This chapter's final section is not intended as philosophy for philosophy's own sake, although I do not think that thealogy should ever apologize for attempting to think through the logic of its beliefs in a rational way. Rather, the following discussion is intended to demonstrate that thealogy's renaming and reconceptualization of the divine present Goddess feminists with philosophical challenges that have significant ethical implications (see further Raphael 1996c: 207-11).

Thealogy thinks about good and evil in highly distinctive ways. Although patriarchy is clearly regarded as a definitively evil political system and world view, thealogians do not generally polarize good and evil as if they were opposing cosmic forces. Thealogians do not postulate the moral perfection of the Goddess. Like nature and the Goddess herself, human situations are usually ambiguous and good and evil are seen as a consequence of complex interactions (Starhawk 1989b: 106).

Where Western patriarchal religion has usually counted death and impermanence as marks of the deficiency of unredeemed nature, thealogy accepts these as necessary and intrinsic to life. Thealogy's cosmogonic myths reflect this in that nature is commonly imaged as generated from the Goddess's body out of pre-existing elements. Birth and death, happiness and loss are all one intermingled, continuously circulating stream of life from which the present forms of nature emerged and to

---

3.   Emily Culpepper has critiqued the all-loving, healing and nurturing thealogy of the 'Great Mother' (1987: 51-71).

which they will return (Raphael 1996b: 262-85). In other words, theal-ogy does not insist that the Goddess created the world out of nothing at all and so can in no sense be held morally responsible for creating an im-perfect world. The imperfect world that is nature does not and cannot yield eternal or perfect human happiness; nor would it make sense to ask the Goddess to intervene to make it do so. Human life is natural, and nature, *as* nature, cannot offer rewards for moral goodness. Although some Goddess feminists I have talked to believe in the reincarnation of the self or the survival of some kind of essence of the self after death, the notion of heavenly or supernatural rewards makes no sense in thealogy. Rather, people pass into and out of personal existence, but even in death remain a part of natural life which is the sum of all that is or can exist.

The 'natural evils' such as disease and natural disasters that cause so much human and animal suffering are a function of the cyclic transfor-mation and renewal of the ecosphere; from a holistic perspective this suffering belongs to a far larger organic cycle which feeds on decay, death and dissolution, but which is, in its totality, good. Thealogy criti-cizes theology for making such cycles the mere scenery of human his-tory and not integral to its substance. For Barbara Walker, the benefit of a thealogical cosmology that envisages the dissolution and regeneration of life as a natural cycle is that it 'makes nonsense' of patriarchy's escha-tological threats and promises' (1988: 112).

This cosmology is an ethical one in so far as it defends the interests and integrity of nature. But thealogy also demonstrates an amoral ten-dency where it represents nature/the Goddess as at once a nurturing and death-dealing divinity who may, in the sheer overwhelming power with which she turns the wheel of life, cause indiscriminate human suffering. Epidemics, tidal waves, tornadoes and volcanic eruptions are all visible, numinous signs of her impersonal natural energy or power. Nonetheless, even if the Goddess Crone or death-dealing aspects are indifferent to human suffering, the Goddess does not *intend* suffering. Natural suffering is not a punishment; it is ecologically intrinsic to life. From a human perspective, impermanence carries loved ones away on its tides, but the tides also carry suffering away and bring in new conditions of possibility: it must be remembered that, in every sense, 'the new moon will rise and that we will shine with it' (Long 1994: 19).

Thealogy has not yet made a substantial contribution to the problem of innocent suffering through the human, moral evil of others. This is probably because it frames its sense of good and evil in a less polarized and more organic way than would most Christians and Jews. Thealogical ethics have centred on the meaning of ethical choice as situated in nature rather than in human reason and doctrinal tradition.

Yet there would be something very bleak about a rigorously ecological response to the problem of innocent suffering (from 'natural evil') were it not that theologians *do* also want to make some more positive claims about the benign nature of the Goddess. She does not incarnate a ruthless indifference to human life; indeed, according to Starhawk, she is not only all that loves and serves life, she also 'needs human help to realize Her fullest beauty' (1982b: 54). Human well-being is as much a part of the Goddess's life and well-being as that of non-human life. Moreover, the necrophilic patriarchal systems under which humans suffer, at the same time diminish her being. In this way, the ethical struggle against human, patriarchal evil can be understood to be thealogically grounded. The human struggle against evil can at the same time be a struggle for the blessings of the immanence of the Goddess.

Certainly, there are times when thealogy's affirmation of the value of nature seems to degenerate into a vitalism that ignores the immediate and pressing needs of vulnerable and oppressed human beings (Raphael 1995: 85-105). However, the struggle to realize the Goddess in her fullness does indicate that there *are* ways in which thealogy transcends mere vitalism and affirms the moral meaning of human life. As one Goddess feminist rightly pointed out, 'unless the Goddess is some type of moral guardian we [spiritual feminists] will not be able to take a firm stand against what is simply not permissible' (Denise 1993: 30). Chapter 2 of this study discussed how Goddess feminism does, in fact, use personalistic images and models of the Goddess, and these help it to engage with moral evil. (As a feminist, and therefore ethical, critique and as a proposed ethical alternative, it cannot *but* engage with human evil.)

Again, although the Goddess does not issue binding norms or laws, this does not that thealogy lacks ethical seriousness. A theological conception of sacred (but still natural) law might be that whatever breaks the web of loving and biological relationships that mend and weave the web of life (namely patriarchy) is absolutely morally wrong. The ecological conception of the world and of the Goddess herself as a web of connections imposes its own practical duties of care. For example, like other contemporary witches, feminist witches have an ethical code which is summarized in the phrase, 'do as you will, as long as it harms none'. This is a far from permissive ethic: it is precisely designed to preserve a balance between individual responsibility, freedom of action and the well-being of the web or whole. Feminist witchcraft also proposes that actions have significant consequences. Its Wiccan 'ethic of three-fold return' warns that a wrong returns with three-fold force on the one who committed it; moral judgment of a sort is part of the very fabric of the cosmos. Although it is rare to find the Goddess petitioned to intervene on humanity's behalf, some Goddess feminists do so. On the Summer Solstice, Zsuszanna Budapest's coven celebrates the Goddess's power—including her power over the might of patriarchy. The festival is an opportunity to bless sons or lovers or put spells on men who have harassed or attacked women. Towards the end of the ritual proceedings the High Priestess intones:

> Great Rhea, Mother of all living, turn the wheel of fortune to the betterment of women and their liberation. You alone have power over patriarchy in this time of oppression . . . Descend upon our enemies in Your fury. Avenge the wrongs, halt the rapes, illuminate the minds of our leaders and judges with your eternal fire. So mote it be! (Budapest 1986: 127-28).

Above all, when Goddess feminists like Starhawk and Wendy Griffin help to stage ritualized, political direct action, they are endeavouring to bring the social community into harmony with the ecological community for the well-being of both. The social and the ecological dimensions are not ultimately distinguishable. This is not only to make the obvious point that social and economic stability will be threatened by environmental instability. It is more that most thealogy does not, in the end, propose that nature is 'blind' or intrinsically amoral, but that it is intelligent and loving (Christ 1997: 156-57). In Starhawk's words,

> Life demands love, because it is through love, of self and others, erotic love, transforming love . . . delighted love for the myriad forms of life evolving and changing, for the redwood and the mayfly, for the blue whale and the snail darter, for wind and sun and waxing moon, caring love for the Cambodian child and the restless ghetto teenager, love of the eternally self-creating world . . . and raging love against all that would diminish the unspeakable beauty of the world, that we connect with the Goddess within and without (1982a: 421).

If, for thealogians, nature is not morally blind, then neither are the Goddess nor Goddess feminists morally indifferent. Although some models of the Goddess as nature's will to survive are less conducive to human ethical and liberative struggle than others, more personalistic models of the Goddess indicate that the Goddess has a concern for the well-being of all living things. If the Goddess is immanent in all living things, then all life is sacred and requires care and protection from harm.

Moreover, while, at present, thealogy's repudiation of institutional authority might make its voice and presence in the global moral forum somewhat difficult to detect, the growing influence of new, extra-governmental social movements may bring thealogy and cognate liberative discourses to greater prominence. Goddess feminism has significant connections with the new social movements for peace, ecological sustainability and sexual and racial equality, that social theorists see as regenerative forces in an overly rationalized, consumerist, hyper-productive late capitalist society.[4] Protest and social change is not only being achieved by violence; it is also beginning to be achieved by non-hierarchical and non-centralized groups that form global networks and movements but whose action is local to the given situation. If this new, organicist method of ethical engagement continues to gather momentum, thealogy may justly understand itself to be within a vanguard whose ethical voice is clear, but whose power has yet to become fully apparent.

4. This point was made by Paul Bowen in his paper, 'The Sense of Goddess: Feminism, Spirituality and Social Theory', given at the Goddess Studies conference, 'Ambivalent Goddesses: An Exploration of the Current State of the Study of Goddesses and Goddess Spirituality', King Alfred's College of Higher Education, 26 March 1997.

Chapter Five

The Politics of Thealogy

> Women whose feminism consists of designing equinox rituals are not viewed in the same light [by secular reformist feminists] as those whose feminism consists of raising a campaign fund for a pro-choice political candidate. One has impeccable feminist credentials; the other has some explaining to do (Eller 1993: 186).

> We have barely tapped the power that is ours. We are more than we know (Spretnak 1982: 398).

Divisions between Spiritual and Secular Feminism

Reformist feminism can be traced back to the eighteenth-century liberal philosophers who argued, in the name of 'the rights of man', that political power should no longer be limited to the monarchy and the aristocracy, but extended to the male property-owning classes (a revolutionary principle at the time). Mary Wollstonecraft's *Vindication of the Rights of Women* (Poston [ed.] 1975) was then to make similar, yet more revolutionary, claims to the full rational, self-determining personhood of women. As radical followers in Wollstonecraft's footsteps were to argue, if women were acknowledged to be fully rational and moral agents there would be no need to deny them the vote. And if women were to be citizens with the vote and the right to hold political office, they would also need to be able to hold property in their own name.

Goddess feminism regards reformist feminism's insistence on women's rights as self-evidently necessary, but not, essentially, transformative. Goddess feminism is a type of radical feminism in claiming that patriarchy summarizes all ideologies—even liberal or 'progressive' ones. All religious and political movements that purport to better the human condition are in Daly's words, 'infra-structures of the edifice of patriarchy' which is '*itself the prevailing religion of the entire planet*, and its essential message is necrophilia' (Daly 1991: 39). This radical feminist view of the patriarchal domination of women as the primal and paradigmatic alienation upon which all other unjust, alienated relations are founded would make women's right to full and equal citizenship no more than a preliminary improvement—a necessity for a tolerable life in a patriarchal culture—but not of ultimate political or spiritual significance. For the most radical of feminists, the women's movement's achievement of legal reforms, rape crisis centres, women's studies programmes and so forth make little *ultimate* difference.

According to Daly, women under patriarchy are bewitched, that is, in a state of robotitude or living death (1991: 55) and must break free/out into the 'Otherworld' in ways that are existential rather than legislative. Although Daly's is a more radical (and perhaps more pessimistic) voice than that of most other spiritual feminists, her basic view that female authenticity is elemental—of nature—and therefore outside or Other to the political process is common to all thealogy. It is not that, as Hester Eisenstein has suggested, Daly's stress on female difference has entailed a withdrawal from political confrontation with patriarchy (1984: 115), but more that the terms on which she and most Goddess feminists fight are themselves wholly Other to those of modern political strategies.

Second Wave radical feminism was, in large part, the fruit of certain feminists splitting away from Marxist and socialist politics in the mid-1960s, on the grounds that feminists should not make alliances with 'progressive' groups who are as blind to their own gender oppressiveness as the reactionaries with whom they are in conflict. The radical feminist rejection of the masculinist revolutionary project was then to take a new turn in the spiritual feminism that grew from that original split.[1]

While Marxist feminism viewed spiritual feminism as indifferent to issues of race, class and economic status, spiritual feminists wanted to

1. This process of political and spiritual differentiation is vividly described in literary form in Starhawk's novel (1997). Starhawk voices the thoughts and feelings of her main protagonist, a Jewish witch named Maya, concerning the difference between a theological and a Marxist approach to achieving social change: 'How could she explain that she didn't want an ideology or a structure for her thoughts, that she was following something intuitive as a scent, as a feeling in her own body that rose up in the presence of freedom. Her critique of what was wrong was not something she could put into a ten-point program. It was a sense of enclosure, a recognition of the deadening of life, that seemed to be generated by structures of thought' (1997: 239).

replace the radical left's doctrines of armed struggle with belief in the power of psychological transformation, ritual and ritualized direct action to change consciousness and, by doing so, begin to change the world. Spiritual feminists experience the women's movement as a spiritual phenomenon—as a manifestation of womanspirit—in itself. On a pragmatic level as well, Zsuszanna Budapest urges that 'Without the Goddess, feminism is not going to work, because you're going to burn out. You've got to have spirituality connected with your political aspiration because that's how this animal [the human being] works' (Bridle 1996: 69).

As Cynthia Eller narrates, the split between secular and spiritual feminism 'began in the early 1970s and peaked in the late 1970s and early 1980s, though it continues to this day'. In its early stages, the conflict was sharpened by the fact that the two factions occupied the same social and political spaces and had discovered feminism together and at the same time. According to Eller, the debate has now cooled considerably. Whilst Zsuszanna Budapest triumphantly claims spiritual feminism as the 'new wave' of feminism, Eller believes that the conflict is simmering rather than boiling simply because 'the two worlds have grown apart' (Eller 1993: 189-91). It is also the case that since the mid 1980s, the rapid growth of Paganism, the New Age Movement and the holistic spiritualities, green politics and alternative medicine that might be said to come under the auspices of the New Age Movement, have all made spiritual feminism seem less culturally and politically marginal than it would have done twenty years ago.

Monica Sjöö and Barbara Mor encapsulate spiritual feminism's political turn in urging their readers to

> Remember that the Great Goddess was always a triplicity; between all dualistic choices, all warring oppositions, stood her being—a third term which mediated and synthesized the polarities into a new thing . . . The whole purpose of studying ancient women's religion and culture is to understand the great precedence for this third term, this third, alternative choice—neither the man's fascism nor the man's communism, but a radical return to the female beginning (Sjöö and Mor 1991: 407).

For Sjöö and Mor, modern patriarchal oppression not only produces inequality but also mechanisation. For them, the political challenge of spiritual feminism can be expressed thus: 'we either rebecome children of the Great Mother, or we remain children of the machine. The opposite of life is not death, *but to become a mechanism*.' This means that,

> Politics is important, social and cultural activity is important, everything
> that can be done should be done to change our situation; but these
> activities cannot extricate us from the machinery if they are still con-
> ducted in the terms of the machinery. Ontological evolution and revo-
> lution must be conducted in the mode of biology-and-the-dream (Sjöö
> and Mor 1991: 390).

Spiritual feminism shares many of the presuppositions and campaigns of
non-religious radical feminism, but its view of women's moral/political
agency is distinctive. That is, its politics are driven by a will to reconnect
with a female elemental power or 'gynergy' that is ultimately Other to
that of masculinist power-politics and, indeed, to the feminine 'power'
or influence claimed by conservative religionists and some nineteenth-
century romantic feminists as that born of maternal, self-sacrificial love.

Spiritual feminist woman-power has moved on from the nineteenth-
century romantic, evangelical feminism (to which it now bears only a
distant family relation). While many of the foremothers of Second Wave
feminism grounded their activism in a Christian mission for the dissem-
ination of maternal and domestic virtues, Goddess feminist activism is
characterized by its confronting patriarchy with the numinous power of
its Otherness. Theirs is a turbulent, primal, 'natural' power often symbolized by the snake, the dragon and the wild horse. It is a power and
authority personified in reclaimed and reconstructed ancient female
numina such as Lilith, the Maenads, the Amazons, Sirens, sybils, witches
and the Crone aspects of the Goddess.

Although patriarchy has always cast the power of such numina as
threatening and chaotic, it would be wrong to suggest that spiritual feminists celebrate evil or violence—they do not. Rather, the invocation of
these numina (who are female but not feminine and whose wills are not
assimilable into Christian or bourgeois norms of feminine duty and obedience) is a sign of Goddess feminists' reclamation of a defiant, ecstatic,
independent, untamed, mysterious pre-patriarchal power.[2]

The use of Pagan numina as standard-bearers in the struggle against
patriarchy is peculiar to the strongly alternative nature of spiritual feminism: most other feminists would find such images of female resistance

---

2.   Useful sources on the historical background of these female numina are
Walker (1983, 1988) and Husain (1994). Books such as Caputi (1993) and Koltuv
(1986) exemplify the spiritual feminist reconstruction of female numina. See also
Raphael (1996b: 183-219).

bizarre and decidedly unhelpful—merely confirming all patriarchal religion's misogynistic superstitions about women and justifying the control of women in the name of morality and good order. For spiritual feminists these numina symbolize whatever is Other and prior to patriarchy, which latter is characterized by violence and devastation. These female numina work their magic as power-names, firing the spiritual/political imagination and marking radical religious feminism's refusal to adapt female power and nature to patriarchal norms; rather, patriarchal norms must adapt (and give way) to theirs.

It is, perhaps, the differences over political and imaginal strategy (even questions of personal temper and taste), not the ultimate liberatory purposes of feminism, that have created antagonism between secular and spiritual radical feminists. Spiritual feminists consider their political approach not only to envision a post-patriarchal future, but to be truly post-patriarchal in its methods of attaining it. For, as Hallie Iglehart observed in 1978, secular feminists are, in effect, subscribing to a primary patriarchal dualism that spiritual feminism has left behind:

> The split between us is created and maintained by patriarchal dualistic concepts of 'spirituality' and 'politics'. It is destructive because it prevents the synthesis of the 'spiritual' and 'political' approaches necessary to establish the kind of world we want to see. When we do make this synthesis within ourselves and within the feminist movement, we will have more power than we ever imagined possible (Iglehart 1982: 405).

As Iglehart goes on to claim, a purely secular, materialist liberation would be a partial liberation, engaging only one aspect of women's oppression. Such a liberation would forget that 'just as material and spiritual oppression go hand in hand, so do political and spiritual power' (1982: 408).

However, secular feminism was not, and is not, persuaded. Spiritual feminist politics is considered a mere diversion; a sedative, unworthy of the name 'politics' at all. Secular feminism continues to focus on the socio-economic struggle for material change. While most Goddess feminists have *also* focused on campaigns for material and legal change, they have done so through the lens and ritual methods of a new spirituality and a new object of religious celebration: the Goddess.

The Political Dimension of Ritual

On the assumption that patriarchy is a dis-spiriting dis-ease that damages the whole web of life, spiritual feminist political transformation is primarily and distinctively understood as healing. For to be healed is to be made whole/holy, and therefore (re)charged with a spiritual and physical power. For this reason, spiritual feminists make spiritual/psychological healing through ritual one of the preconditions of political empowerment. This means that all forms of healing—including that of private trauma—contribute to the renewal of women's energy to effect personal and, at the same time, political change. In this way, religious ritual, which is the means by which a religion makes its sphere holy or whole, attains a political status.[3]

Goddess feminists have not been alone in their concern to develop rituals that address the emotional/spiritual needs of women, as perceived by women not men, and that are articulated and performed in non-masculinist language and contexts. Feminist rituals and liturgies have also been the life-blood of Jewish and Christian feminism.[4] Focusing the ritual or liturgy on women's lives and need for self-expression is itself a political act: a way of coming to share a means to the sacred power of healing and transformation once monopolized by male officiants.

It is little wonder, then, that rituals have a particular centrality in Goddess feminism. This is because Goddess feminists subscribe to forms of magical thinking (even when they are not witches) and there need be no absolute distinction made between the transformation and renewal effected by ritual and that effected by political action. As Starhawk explains:

> If magic is 'the art of causing change in accordance with will', then political acts, acts of protest and resistance, acts that speak truth to power, that push for change, are acts of magic . . . I once defined a spell as 'a symbolic act done in a deepened state of consciousness'. When political action moves into the realm of symbols, it becomes magical. If we apply the principles of magic to politics, we can understand political actions better and make them more effective (Starhawk 1990a: 169).

So, for example, when Goddess women surround a nuclear installation—a natural space occupied and desecrated by patriarchal destructive power—their chanting, web-weaving and other non-violent direct actions magically name and will an Other, non-patriarchal, reality and

---

3.   Donna Read's film *Full Circle*, Great Atlantic and Pacific Film Company and the National Film Board of Canada, 1992, is an invaluable record of Goddess feminism's politicization of ritual.

4.   Such texts are too numerous to list here, but see, e.g., Orenstein (1994: I).

infuse the profaned site with purifying, biophilic, sacred female energy (see, e.g., Starhawk 1990a: 168-80).

As a rule, Goddess feminists engage ritually and practically with political issues, rather than through the formulation of new ideological abstractions. The Journeywoman Clan of West Yorkshire, for example, is a non-aligned group of self-styled witches who generate energy to confront issues of sexual violence against women through their ritual relations and offerings to the land.[5] Thealogical texts and practitioners offer a vast array of collective and solitary rituals that are gynocentric and concerned with events and desires that patriarchy has considered to be outside the proper sphere of both religion and politics. These include rites of passage celebrating the changing energies of the body such as at menarche or menopause (Holbrook 1983: 36), especially as these correlate with the changing energies of the land which are marked by the festivals of the Pagan year (Budapest 1989: 113-54). Spell-casting, pathworking or shamanic journeying are also used to help women to overcome feelings of powerlessness or despair (Starhawk 1990: 45-71). Group rituals bond women together as sisters and raise a collective energy that is greater than the numerical sum of its participants. Some rituals invoke the assistance of the Goddess and others do not.

Rituals are also used to 'work through' personally traumatic experiences such as rape or divorce. Heather Whiteside, for example, designed a triad of rituals invoking the wisdom of the goddess Sophia to help her come to terms with her divorce. These were a ritual of self affirmation, a herbal charm to heal her 'broken heart', and a three-day candle spell to ease the pain of separation. She writes that it was 'through symbolic enactments and rituals that I [began] to clear my mind and life of the past' (Young 1993: 431). One of Goddess feminism's best-known solitary rituals is Zsuzsanna Budapest's Wiccan Self-Blessing Ritual in which a woman makes time and space to honour her own divinity. The Self-Blessing Ritual is 'a way of exorcising the patriarchal policeman, cleansing the deep mind, and filling it with positive images of the strength and beauty of women' (Christ and Plaskow 1992: 272). In short, all ritual practices are interconnected as ways of unblocking obstructions to the flow of relational energy that fosters human and planetary health.

5.   I have withheld references for this group. Although they have publicized their work among like-minded spiritual feminists, they would probably not wish to be the objects of non-feminist research.

However, many influential spiritual feminists do not consider ritual alone as a sufficient political end in itself. For Riane Eisler (as for Starhawk, who is particularly active in the American anti-nuclear movement), ritual must be integrated with social action. Mere ritual alone would amount to little more than, 'dancing in the woods. Goddess rituals do change our consciousness and help us to bond, but if we stop there, it is like fireworks, which quickly dissipate' (Eisler 1995a: 23). Secular radical feminists, however, see spiritual feminist ritual as just that: flamboyant gestures without any grounding in political change. The gulf between a religio-magical world view and a secular materialist one does not appear to be traversable.

The Place of Men in Thealogy

While criticized for including and essentializing all womankind in its discursive ambit, regardless of women's evident social and ethnic differences, Goddess feminism is also criticized for being (or appearing to be) exclusive of men, regardless of evident political and spiritual difference among them. Ursula King has justly remarked, 'What is certain, a religion for women alone is not enough to change the social and political distribution of power in the contemporary world'. She suggests that there is a greater need for a new holistic religion for women *and* men which does not 'practice a kind of sexism in reverse' by replacing the absolute pre-eminence of God with that of the Goddess (1989: 150, 153).

It is true that if Goddess religion intended to be a religion for women alone it could never finally engage the hearts and minds of any but those women with a predisposition for separatism. But it seems to me that all but separatists invite and welcome the participation of men in Goddess religion so long as they affirm its anti-patriarchal stance. In fact, many critics overplay thealogy's separatism and gynocentrism. (Mary Daly's views leave her somewhat on her own in this regard.) Carol Christ's attitude is probably typical of most Goddess feminists:

> Though I write about women's experiences and Goddesses, I do not deny the validity of men's experiences (when they are not deformed by patriarchal assumptions), nor do I deny that Goddess/God may *also* be imaged as male. I write of women's experiences and Goddesses for the simple reason that I write what I know (Christ 1987: x-xi).

For Christ, 'As men become more involved in childbirth and child care, new images of sacred nurturing fathers can emerge to complement images of birth-giving Goddesses' (Christ 1997: 95). In the meantime, she acknowledges the difficulties some women will experience in celebrating fatherhood and the phallus in the same way as they would motherhood and the womb. This is because 'in our world, too many have experienced fathers as dominating others and the phallus as an instrument of rape. New images can only emerge as men and culture change' (1997: 95).

Admittedly, among other Goddess feminists there is often too close an association of maleness and patriarchy, as if patriarchy were a biological or ontological condition rather than a destructive and exploitative world view and political system. After all, if patriarchy is an ontological or essential quality of masculinity—that which defines masculinity—there is little left to hope for. But to some extent any spiritual/political programme for change will also address and change men, even if only implicitly or indirectly. If a programme for political change only affects women's lives it is a change so partial as hardly to qualify as the paradigm-shifting spiritual politics Goddess feminists are trying to develop.

Perhaps it is not so much that men's spirituality is denied, as that thealogy is simply a very new discourse, determined to give women their voice after millennia of customary silence. The opportunity for women to conduct public religious discourse has only very recently come into being and it is still working for independence from masculine institutional authority. Thealogy's articulation of its relevance for men has, understandably, not been a priority. If, over time, men's commitment to feminist values increases, this will probably change. The role of men and male symbolism in Goddess religion will gradually be given more careful consideration and incorporated into thealogical discourse and practice on a more equivalent footing (Christ 1987: 69-71). Few would wish to simply turn the tables on men by establishing a religion that practically and discursively excludes them. Carol Christ affirms this: 'I believe that men also need the Goddess, and I hope they will write more about their experience' (1987: 111).

Not all men would wish to do so. Some factions within the men's movement are part of a backlash against the women's movement and are anxious for the psychological well-being of men in a post-colonial, post-industrial age. These men are fighting a rearguard action for cultural values and spirituality that are distinctively masculine in character.

Patrick Arnold, for example, regards 'the burgeoning field of Goddess religion' as having particular responsibility for a feminist misandry, that has been (in his witchburner's idiom) 'bubbling away on the back-burners of resentful women like a Poison Stew . . . Men are ingesting these misandrist toxins, usually unknowingly, and feeling unwell'. Arnold celebrates the Bronze Age shift from the worship of the 'static feminine' to the 'dynamic masculine' and feels that Goddess feminists should recognize and accept that the Goddess was, at this time, properly supplanted by masculine deities who met the spiritual needs of ancient cultures far more effectively than could the Goddess (Arnold 1992: 52-57).

Other men have a quite different attitude. They are involved in the Goddess movement as Goddess feminists, other kinds of Pagans, and participants in the anti-patriarchal men's movement. The kind of men in the men's movement who are open to the Goddess are usually those who are pro-feminist and seek to learn from a feminist analysis of patriarchy. They acknowledge that the patriarchal system damages not only women and nature, but men as well. For feminist men of a post-Christian disposition, the Goddess can be an essential part of their experience of the men's movement and its search for a holistic spirituality and for healing from the wounds patriarchy inflicts on men themselves by the culture of machismo.

In *The Horned God: Feminism and Men as Wounding and Healing*, John Rowan argues that the Goddess is as important for men as she is for women. He believes that men must 'question patriarchy at the deepest and most serious level'; it was the Goddess who helped him to do so. Finding the Goddess was, he says, like 'finding a long-lost mother' (1987: 83). When he first read Starhawk's *The Spiral Dance* he was overwhelmed by a 'shock of recognition'. Rowan was particularly influenced by Starhawk and Monica Sjöö; he writes: 'because I had learned about her from feminist women, it was not a male and flattering image of the Goddess that I had, but a strong female vision of the Goddess' (1987: 77). Indeed, Rowan's poem about the Goddess could equally have been written by a woman:

> My heart, Her heart now, singing, wide open, all full
> All full of Her
> Her darkness, Her blood, Her power, Her changes
> Her force, Her awe, Her strength, Her depth . . .
> All filling me now (Rowan 1987: 77).

It may be that for a while longer at least Goddess feminist spirituality will draw particularly on women's voices, women's traditional occupations and their ways of caring and being intimate with others. However, the religious feminist principle of the interconnectedness of all living things must, if it is to be meaningful, also come to apply to its connections with men, especially men who, like Rowan, want to embody or adopt 'female' modes of relation: 'Only after males can appreciate and affirm women and women's culture, only after males realize that they might yet learn something about life from females, can true reconciliation be achieved between them' (Collins 1982: 367). Such a view assumes that patriarchy need have no biological basis; men can learn from women's example. In sum, the affirmative discussion of masculinity may be largely absent from thealogical discourse, but men are addressed and challenged, even if only by implication, in all thealogical discourse. Traditions of 'women-only' Goddess groups and publications still exist, but Starhawk's inclusive, non-separatist attitude has allowed her work to become more influential among alternative religionists than that of any other spiritual feminist.

The Post–Patriarchal Vision

At a meeting in Bristol on 10 January 1993, the British radical feminist Goddess group, Amma Mawu,[6] took the deliberately absurdist step of declaring that the beginning of the 'End of Patriarchy' was to take place at midnight—the witching hour—of 1-2 August 1993, on Silbury Hill in Wiltshire. Tarot readings had indicated that the auspicious year 2000 was to be the year of the High Priestess and this suggested to some spiritual feminists that patriarchy should be over by the millennium. One in the group, Rachel, a traveller, felt that 'the end' could be set in train without delay.

The declaration of the End of Patriarchy reveals a great deal about the religio-political methods of spiritual feminists. What is notable about this declaration is, on the one hand, its playful parody of religious millenarianism, and on the other, its prophetic seriousness. To declare the End of Patriarchy is, in one sense, madness—patriarchy is quite evidently not

6.   'Amma' is 'a basic name of the Great Goddess of the East; it also has many meanings related to the Mother in many different languages. Mawu is the African Mother Goddess who creates all life and is the source of the universe' (anonymous editorial, *From the Flames* 9 [1993]: 6).

in a state of imminent collapse, let alone over. If it were, the end would more likely have been brought about by the decimation of the human species in a global war or ecological catastrophe than by the contemporary women's movement. So too, the methods of notifying the world to this momentous end time event were far from sensible: daubing graffiti, wearing sandwich-boards, stickers, issuing invitation cards and faxes to multinationals and other patriarchal institutions were just a few of those suggested. But even though declaring the End of Patriarchy was an occasion for parties and Tricksterish behaviour,[7] this was a sacred madness. Religious meaning and power was released in the process of naming —even fictioning—the End of Patriarchy. 'Acting from your own truth rather than within the frame of what is officially allowed/tolerated' was, in the experience of those who conceived the event, profoundly revitalizing and empowering. This was, after all, calling

> upon the power of the spoken word, the magic of Naming, Declaring and Proclaiming—usually a prerogative of power. In doing this . . . we are invoking the age-old powerful magic of spells and chants, incantations and affirmations; we are also taking on our own Power, asserting our right to Name the Reality we wish to bring into being . . . It's clear to me that if we Declare the End of Patriarchy at Lammas Full Moon, we may not suddenly wake up to find it gone . . . but something will have changed . . . something shifted . . . inside the world and inside ourselves . . . in some way things will never be the same again.[8]

Silbury Hill, from which the group proposed to witness the dawning of the post-patriarchal age, is a sacred site dated from about 4500 BCE. According to those in the Goddess movement at least, it is the oldest surviving image of the Goddess in Europe. The Hill depicts the Goddess squatting in the Neolithic birthing position, ready to give birth to the

---

7.   A Trickster is a figure common in the world's religions, particularly in the Pagan traditions. The Trickster is elusive, shape shifting, and undertakes cunning, crazy, subversive exploits, often for the purpose of outwitting the dominant deities.

8.   This quotation and the account of the plans for Declaring the End of Patriarchy are from Veronica MacIntyre's contribution to a piece of collective writing (MacIntyre et al. 1993: 4-5). Needless to say, this declaration was met with some scepticism by others allied with spiritual feminism. See Jean (no surname given) (1993: 15): 'Sometime way back a month or two, I spent a weekend sitting round a smokey camp fire eating vegan stew talking to my friends, and lammas night on Silbury hill under a full moon and some wimmin said they were declaring the end of patriarchy. Oh? So wots all this then that I'm coping with? . . . Is this patriarchy thrashing about in its death throes? I doubt it.'

harvest. Until the late seventeenth century, the rural community (and especially the witches) would experience Lammas Eve (1 August), as a cosmic drama that was played out under a full moon. By about 4.30 am the child/harvest was born as the sunrise cast its light over the Hill: the Goddess's body (Ozaniec 1993: 167-71; Sjöö and Mor 1991: 104-105).

It was here at Silbury Hill in 1993, that, in the tradition of the witches who once gathered at Silbury on Lammas Eve, Goddess women sang, drummed and danced as the sun set, the new moon rose, and the sun rose again over the birth of a new social reality. For some, like Albatross who movingly describes lying pregnant and naked in the moonlight on the 'pregnant' mound of Silbury Hill, the event combined the personal and the political in ways characteristic of spiritual feminism at its most religiously effective. In her account of the event, Albatross describes how her own declaration of the end of patriarchy was not intended literally, but was rather to send out a 'ripple' into women's consciousness and imagination; it was a 'glimpse' of what freedom could be like; not a denial of the real and continuing struggle against patriarchy (1993: 13-14).

However post-patriarchy might be achieved, few spiritual feminists would claim that a post-patriarchal society would simply eradicate suffering—rather, that it would begin to undo five-thousand-year-old structures of domination, exploitation and gratuitous suffering. A spiritual feminist world would not be a perfect one because it would be a natural one and nature is not perfect. But it *would* be a global community whose organizational structures, spiritual values and material priorities would deprive patriarchal elites of their very conditions of possibility.

The thealogical utopia is not a mere futurist day-dream, but envisions a society based on the full realization and universalization of embryonic elements of politics and practices already present in alternative political, spiritual, and technological circles. The 'New Political Agenda' recently disseminated by Starhawk on her World-Wide Web page articulates a spiritual politics that intends to include as broad a spectrum of political and religious progressives as possible. Her vision is not addressed to feminist Pagans alone (indeed it is not explicitly premised on celebration or worship of the Goddess at all) but offers a 'five-point agenda' under the headings of 'sacred values, diversity, self-determination, environment, human needs and social justice' in the hope that a variety of local and global spiritual/political alliances can be built on a foundation of spirituality, freedom, ecological sustainability, human fulfilment, the celebration of human difference and the redressing of social inequalities.[9]

To take another example, Riane Eisler's two best known works, *The Chalice and the Blade: Our History, Our Future* and the later *Sacred Pleasure: Sex, Myth and the Politics of the Body* both exemplify a spiritual feminist view of the socio-political effects of a spirituality of connection. Whereas traditional spirituality entails self-abegnation and some form of physical or emotional separation from the world, in *The Chalice and the Blade* Eisler develops a model of what she calls a 'partnership' (feminist) society. In this society the holding of power is symbolized by the womb-like properties of the regenerative, protective, 'female' chalice or grail. Partnership societies, as opposed to 'dominator' (patriarchal) societies symbolized by the sharpened blade, link rather than rank all living things. 'Partnership' societies put spirituality at the heart of politics as a public necessity rather than a private vocation. Eisler has since established a Center for Partnership Studies in the United States to promote these ideas. Nor are such ideas peculiar to Eisler's world view: the Creation Spirituality movement and the spiritual wing of the green movement would be in substantial agreement.

If, by now, the reader is wondering how post-patriarchal politics would translate into an actual lifestyle for the future, the following sketch might suffice. Clearly, not every Goddess feminist would subscribe to every element I have noted, some would list elements I might have overlooked and some have already lived in communities where some of these elements have been realized. Crucially, in a post-patriarchal utopia, spiritual feminist communities would take different forms the world over. Even so spiritual feminism intends its values and practices to be of global, not only local, relevance.

For many Goddess feminists, post-patriarchal communities would be religiously plural, but primarily Goddess-honouring. They would be egalitarian, collectivist rather than individualist, non-racist, non-tribalist, non-heterosexist, non-speciesist and without warfare. Death would not be feared, but accepted and celebrated as a natural precondition of ecological renewal.

It is not that spiritual feminists want to return to a pre-technological stone age. But a new Goddess-honouring, matrifocal culture would probably be without large-scale industrial production and would practise

---

9.   Starhawk 1995: 2-7. The web page address is http://www.reclaiming.org/cauldron.

ecologically sensitive and appropriate technologies. The economy would be locally rather than transnationally organized and would be characterized by greatly reduced consumption, with a mix of cooperative trade, barter, the recycling of materials and gift-giving. Technology and the production of goods would be reconceived and practised as craft. Technology would have contemporary elements but would also recall the cosmogonic 'technologies' of the Goddess as she (mythopoeically speaking) spun, wove, cooked, planted and brewed life into being. Nurturing occupations traditionally practised by women such as motherhood, cooking, sewing, gardening, midwifery, holistic medicine and so forth would become social priorities. Artists, poets, healers, visionaries, oracles, diviners, mothers and grandmothers would be especially valued, but, without any social hierarchy, that respect would bestow no special privileges.

In these post-patriarchal communities, women would have the ultimate say over their reproductive choices and sexual identities would be far more fluid than patriarchal sexual ideology presently permits. Although a minority of spiritual feminist separatists might prefer to imagine a feminist utopia without men, for the majority of spiritual feminists, a post-patriarchal society would invite the full and equal participation of men who had relinquished their patriarchal privileges and powers. Clearly, many, perhaps most, of the elements of this utopian vision would be shared by large numbers of men and women on the alternative political and religious left. It is really only the gynocentric emphases of Goddess worship and the revaluation of female modes of production and reproduction that are distinctively thealogical, though these would undoubtedly shape the spiritual politics of such a community in important ways.

In Britain, the 'Women's Spiral Camps' organized by various groups of 'spiral women' over recent summers have offered a kind of free Goddess festival and represent a foretaste of some aspects of the spiritual feminist utopia. In the words of an advertisement for the 1993 Spiral Camp, 'The camp welcomes women of all sexualities and all ethnic backgrounds, to develop an open forum for discussion, political debate, empowerment, the celebration of nature and the celebration of women as sacred, spiritual and healer [sic]'. Usually about 300 women and their children attend these camps.

However, in 1996 a confrontation between the Goddess women of the Spiral Camp and those of the Glastonbury Goddess Conference

crystallized the difference between utopias and present—far from ideal—
realities. Here, when women from the Spiral Camp 'gatecrashed' the
closing banquet of the 1996 Goddess Conference, the British Goddess
feminist community showed itself to be riven by class difference, or at
least a perception of class difference. The women of the Spiral Camp,
were angry that they could not afford the ticket for the banquet and,
casting themselves as the 'Bad Faeries' of European mythological tradition, they decided to stage a piece of political theatre by dressing up,
forming a carnival procession of their own and invading the Assembly
Rooms where the banquet was to be held. However, while many at the
conference welcomed their unexpected guests, others found the 'inva-
sion' unnecessarily aggressive, divisive and distressing for children who
were present.[10]

In fact, many of the women who attended the Goddess conference
were on government benefits, very low incomes, or had been given
complimentary tickets in return for a lecture, performance, cooking or
other contribution. The polarization between 'rich' and 'poor' Goddess
women was, to some degree, a false one.[11] And yet in some respects, the
women of the Spiral Camp were right to perceive a division in the
Goddess movement. This is less an economic division than a division of
political commitment. Although this book has focused on Goddess *feminism*, many Goddess feminists would agree that in other parts of the
Goddess movement its original political dynamic is in decline or is being
weakened by New Age and mainstream Pagan influences. There are
now conferences and Goddess gatherings which explicitly distance themselves from the feminist movement. There are also many in the movement who are turning the Goddess into the kind of female or 'feminine'
divinity who, as the apex of the cosmic hierarchy of being, is perceived
as having power over humanity in ways that are hardly feminist in character.[12]

10. For a detailed commentary on this event, and one which publishes the views
of both the Spiral Women and the Goddess women attending the conference, see
From the Flames 18 (1996): 29-34.

11. The common charge that Goddess feminists are predominately white and
prosperous is at most a half truth. Most Goddess feminists may be white, but they
are not necessarily monied. Goddess women do not have equal access to experience
of the Goddess through Goddess tours and workshops, the cost of which is pro-
hibitive for many.

12. Ruth Mantin, an academic with a particular research interest in the Goddess
movement, made these latter two points at Lucy Lepchani's workshop, 'Goddess

Many Goddess feminists would agree that time has moved on and the radicalism and collectivism of the period in which the Goddess movement was born is giving way to the individualism and the privatization of spirituality that is characteristic of the present period. If this is the case, the Goddess movement will, perhaps not irrevocably, move away from its radical feminist roots and further towards a spirituality of self-actualization.

Certainly, contemporary Goddess talk is not always politically aware or helpful. There are teachers and writers in the Goddess movement who appear politically lightweight to say the least. For example, at the 1997 Goddess Conference in Glastonbury, a presentation called 'Grace of the Giving Goddess' was given by Edwene Gaines from Alabama during which she urged the praise of the Goddess in an evangelical, revivalist style. With a warmth and sincerity that many women clearly found moving, she assured her audience that the Goddess is a 'giving' Goddess who responds if we 'open our hearts' and 'make a commitment' to her. For Gaines, (whose dress, heavy make-up and coiffed hair was more redolent of the Christian far right than the Goddess feminist left) the Goddess wants women to change the world by *'feminine* consciousness' (stress mine). Gaines does not appear to be thinking in terms of feminist activism here: women can have the prosperity and happy life they desire if they simply believe that the Goddess provides an abundance for all.

Paritosh Peachey also exemplifies a Goddess woman in whose words one can hear merely the reverberations of feminism, not feminism itself. In Peachey's publicity there is recognition that women are not 'whole', but her work lacks a real political context or purpose. Peachey's weekend workshops offer a 'rite of passage into Womanhood' and are advertised as providing 'a safe, nurturing and supportive space to come and explore your inner being'. Healing, peace and fulfilment are personal rather than global; the Goddess becomes the source of 'our full potential as Women', not primarily of a world politically and environmentally at peace with itself. Similarly, Karen LaPuma (1991) uses the Goddess psychotherapeutically as an instrument of self-improvement. Whilst LaPuma concedes that global change is necessary, she insists that such change is, essentially, a product of positive thinking (of a rather self-interested kind). Her Goddess spirituality appears to have been shaped not by

Politics—Working Where We Are', at the Glastonbury Goddess Conference, 9 August 1997.

feminist politics, but by patriarchal depth psychology and Eastern mysticism. She suggests the use of a 'mantra' to be repeated 'over and over again' and which suggests that transformation can be achieved by focusing on 'what you want to *become*, not on what you want to *overcome*'. Using a form of self-hypnosis, Goddess women are to say:

> Every day, in every way, I get better and better.
> I am Light, I am Love, and I am Goddess.
> I am healthy, wealthy and wise.
> I am open to receive all that is good for me . . . (LaPuma 1991: 57).

In the early days of Goddess feminism, it seemed almost a truism to say that the personal, political and spiritual dimensions were one and that each implied the other; now, sometimes, it can seem as if the fulfilment of the personal and the spiritual dimensions is a sufficient end in itself. Even as significant a thealogian as Carol Christ finds herself at times personally disenchanted with and 'betrayed' by the feminist movement. For her, feminism had held out the promise that she could 'have it all': career, children and family, but, in the end, delivered none of them (Christ 1995: 52).

But it seems to me that Asphodel Long and all those other Goddess feminists who see the Goddess as central to the dynamics of the women's movement, are wholly correct in understanding the very heart and purpose of Goddess feminism and its thealogy to be political. These feminists are passionately convinced that the recovery of the Goddess is a primary act of political justice. If the erasure of the female divine also spells the erasure of human female power and worth, then to resurrect the Goddess is to resurrect female power in its most comprehensive and inviolable form. Certainly, female divinities and the oppression of women coexist in Hinduism and throughout the world where goddesses are still worshipped. But the *feminist* revival of Goddess religion sets the Goddess in the emancipatory context of Western late modernity. Here the secular, egalitarian values of the liberal Enlightenment tradition reconfigure the meaning of the Goddess, just as she reconfigures the values of modernity. The Goddess of Goddess feminism is not simply a composite of the goddesses of the world's Pagan traditions; while she bears some of their names she is, above all, the meta-patriarchal and post-patriarchal Goddess of liberation.

Chapter Six

Feminist Witchcraft

I do mean witch. The heretic who rejects the idols of patriarchy is the blasphemous creatrix of her own thoughts. She is finding her life and intends not to lose it (Daly 1975: 29).

Who and What is a Witch?

Not all Goddess religionists are witches and some are quite hostile to magical practice (see King 1989: 138-42). Feminist witches or Wiccans, however, celebrate the Goddess and seek to embody her power through witchcraft. Feminist Wicca is a specific and substantial sub-group within the broad category of Goddess religion and constitutes a (primarily) women's religion that is, in its present form, about 25 years old. Feminist Wicca is a political variant of mainstream neo-Pagan Wicca and it incorporates a fusion of feminist and green politics, shamanic and psychotherapeutic techniques and 'folk' medicine within a Goddess celebrating, magical worldview. Like other Wiccans, feminist Wiccans belong to covens, or may, by temperament or circumstance, practice alone as 'solitaries'. In 1989 it was claimed that feminist witchcraft is 'relatively rare in England, but quite important in the States' (Luhrmann 1994: 54). But judging by the number of feminist Wiccan texts currently available in British bookshops, interest in feminist Wicca is increasing.

Although feminist Wicca is a discrete grouping within the Goddess worshipping community, rarely is a rigid *thealogical* or philosophical distinction upheld between Wiccan feminists and other Goddess feminists. A magical world view is held more or less in common by witches and non-witches, and books published by feminist Wiccans like Starhawk are as influential within the wider spiritual feminist community as they are for feminist Wiccans themselves. The magical concepts and practices I describe under the auspices of this chapter are not, then, confined to self-defined witches. For example, Carol Christ is not a witch and yet in earlier times (which she now recalls with 'nostalgia' and 'gratitude' [Christ 1997: 42]) she contributed a section called 'Rituals for Daily Life' to Zsuszanna Budapest's witchcraft manual. Here celebrations of the presence of the Goddess in Christ's life are referred to as 'spells' which give her strength in times of weakness, and magnify her strength when she feels empowered (Budapest 1986: 71-72). Although her concept of the Goddess is noticeably less 'Trinitarian' than that of feminist Wiccans, Christ raises power in a circle, celebrates the cycles of the seasons and the moon and has been inspired by the two best known feminist witches, Starhawk and 'Z' (Zsuszanna Budapest) (Christ 1987: 108-109). Similarly, D.J. Conway's *Maiden, Mother, Crone* does not advertise itself as a Wiccan manual, but it offers models for rituals with a 'magickal purpose' which are virtually indistinguishable from Wiccan rituals and which use Wiccan ritual paraphernalia (1994: 151). Or again, Mary Daly is not a Wiccan as such, but understands the purpose of her book *Gyn/Ecology* as 'nothing less than the transformation of tamed women into Wild Witches' (Daly 1993: 224). While writing *Gyn/Ecology*, Daly used 'a Witch's Self-determining Spell':

> The words, as I Re-Call them, were 'no matter what happens to me afterwards (or as a consequence) I WILL write this book.' This spell carried me through the dark nights of my soul's Journey and onward into more Be-Dazzling adventures (1993: 214).

Many, if not most, Goddess feminists report a sense that they 'knew' the Goddess from childhood, even before they heard her named (Christ 1997: 1). Similarly, most witches report a cognate sense of having always been a witch 'without really knowing what the word meant' (Starhawk 1997: 346). For Daly, as for many spiritual feminists, any woman who has spiritually liberated herself from the patriarchal world view is, essentially, a witch even if she does not (yet) call herself one. A feminist witch may be defined as a woman who is (once more) 'in harmony with the rhythms of the universe' (Daly 1984: 90). As Monica Sjöö and Barbara Mor put it,

> The wiccan nature, or witchcraft, is the original nature of all women, deriving from our primary biological experience, our psychic relationship with the earth and cosmos. It is this experience, this relationship, that patriarchy sets out to destroy (1991: 207).

Any woman who 'bows to no man' is a threat to patriarchal power: a witch by both patriarchal and spiritual feminist definition. The idea of the feminist as, essentially, a witch was not invented by spiritual feminists themselves. As far back as Halloween 1968 a group of New York radical feminists, among them Robin Morgan, styled themselves as witches or, more accurately, WITCH—an acronym originally standing for 'Women's International Terrorist Conspiracy from Hell'. WITCH covens quickly spread to other states. WITCH was far from being an earth-based women's mystery religion, or indeed any religion, but was something of an anarchic sisterhood enjoining a theatrical form of feminist praxis. WITCH's targets were centres of financial, academic and corporate power. WITCH was based on an idea of women who, like witches and gypsies, 'were the original guerillas and resistance fighters against oppression—particularly the oppression of women—right down the ages'. The secular radical feminist witch was 'a total concept of revolutionary female identity', whose Manifesto claimed that witches have always been the intelligent, sexually liberated, nonconformist, courageous women of their generations. And potentially, 'WITCH lives and laughs in every woman. She is the free part of each of us'. In lines routinely quoted in spiritual feminist texts, WITCH urged women to claim their own power: 'You are a witch by saying aloud, "I am a Witch" three times, and *thinking about that*. You are a witch by being female, untamed, angry, joyous, and immortal' (Morgan 1982: 427, 429).

The sense that a witch is a woman who calls patriarchy to account was dramatically enacted in an event called 'The Witches Return' that took place on Sunday 14 May (Mother's Day) 1989 in the Sanders Theatre at Harvard University. 'The Witches Return' was organized by Mary Daly with a number of her 'Cronies' and students—'the Witches of Boston'. This drama was an ironic reversal of the old witch trials; now radical feminism would judge the gynocidal patriarchs. There were seven categories of gynocidal criminal put on (theatrical) trial. Among these were pornographers, serial killers, 'Earth-rapers', academic 'brain-drainers' and the Roman Catholic hierarchy. All of these were proven guilty, hexed or cursed 'with force and fury', and ritually executed by 'de-heading'. During the proceedings Daly pronounced a 'Nemesis Hex': 'For peace and love we ever yearned / but some do wrong and never learn. / This time it won't be us that burn / the wrath of Nemesis is here!' Daly also conjured the elemental powers of Earth, Air, Fire and

Water and the presence of foresisters such as Joan of Arc and Sojourner Truth (1993: 395-98).

Magic is most commonly defined by spiritual feminists as the art of changing reality at will; it is, as Donate Pahnke puts it, the 'fundamental connecting *Weltanschauung* [world view] and life-practice of feminist spirituality'. And Pahnke goes further, claiming that even where 'the "religion" of the Goddess goes beyond [magic] by representing a myth-ical-theological superstructure', nonetheless,

> the affiliation to feminist spirituality is not primarily expressed through the belief in the Goddess or in a mythical superstructure, nor through formally joining a movement or denomination, nor by following a pro-phetic authority, but its determining characteristic is the decision for a life-practice of 'magic' as the art of changing consciousness and reality at will (King 1995: 172).

It seems clear, then, that in thealogy, witchcraft need not be a discrete religion but can be a political statement and a psycho-spiritual orien-tation. In particular, magic as 'strong wishing' permeates the whole of Goddess religion. As Naomi Goldenberg notes, 'Goddess religion can often appear as "wish-craft" because it teaches women to use spells and rituals to express their hopes, ambitions and desires'. And as we saw in Chapter Three, 'wish-craft' even permeates its historiographical method: 'sometimes the idea of a matriarchy in the past is put forward as a wish about history—a desire to be realized in the present and future'. In fact, as Goldenberg recognizes, this is not untypical of religion as a whole. While its methods for realizing the personal and cosmic good is dis-tinctive, Goddess religion is hardly alone among the world's religions in its striving for the good: 'just as all others, [Goddess religion] is based around wishes and hopes for power, comfort, influence, and justice' (Goldenberg 1995: 155-56). Even so, conservative scholarship and religious culture would not accept that there is any common ground between feminist witches and other religionists. Crude demonization of Wiccan religion, as well as a priori definitions of what properly constitutes religion have all contributed to a widespread refusal to accept Western witchcraft (let alone feminist witchcraft) as a legitimate religion or legitimate object of study (Goldenberg 1979: 109-11, 114; Roney-Dougal 1991: 202; Ruether 1976: 93).

The Patriarchal Idea of a Witch

'Witches', according to Sharukh Husain,

> have been part of every known culture since the dawn of time, casting
> spells, healing the wounded and spinning fate. Even before recorded
> time, they became identified almost immutably with death and evil. The
> first extant mythology (circa 3000 BC) found on Sumerian tablets tells of
> an exiled witch-goddess—stern, cold and pitiless—ruling the Underworld
> like her later counterparts such as Demeter (Husain 1994: xiii).

Even at the end of the twentieth century, the noun 'witch' still evokes
salacious curiosity and a numinous shudder. The contemporary Western
idea of a witch differs little from that of the late mediaeval period,
described by Husain as,

> an unwashed and unkempt woman with long, dirty fingernails, mucoid
> eyes and decaying teeth. She had hair in unattractive places—sprouting
> out of her nose, ears or chin. Her voice was shrill, squeaky or cracked.
> Her skin was blemished with moles and sores believed to be inflicted by
> the suckling of imps and devils . . . She was surrounded by bats, toads,
> rats, crows and malevolent cats (1994: xvi).

Although modernity does not profess belief in evil spirits, the patriarchal
image of a witch captures the imagination of contemporary children as
much as it ever did. And whilst children's mythology of witches omits
the old view of the witch as sexually active, draining men of their
semen/strength and copulating with goats and the devil, the ancient and
globally attested cannibal witch survives in fairly tales like that of the
child-eating witch in the story of Hansel and Gretel.

The patriarchal idea of a witch image concentrates centuries of misogyny. Even the beautiful witch is, beneath the skin, as putrescent as the
hag witch. Her seductive beauty is merely a shape shifter's mask used to
lure men into her abysmal power, leaving chaos and destruction in her
wake and so, like Eve, helping Christian ideologues to justify the
subjugation of all women. This witch has been an anti-type of Christian
virtue—especially that of the Catholic priest. Rather than bringing good
moral order to a community—as would a celibate priest—her power
was sexual and disordering. Whereas her power was sold secretly to her
clientele from her dark and cobweb-strewn home on the edge of the
community, the priest lived in austere purity in the midst of his congregants, sacrificing his needs to theirs. The patriarchal idea of a witch is

one who is vengeful rather than just and above all, she is obedient to the devil where the priest is obedient to God.

In short, patriarchy has told stories about strong, knowledgeable women in such a way as to intimidate other women. Feminists would not deny that genuinely malign women have existed and do exist. Rather, historically, patriarchal religion has cast *any* powerful woman as dangerous or evil and as one whose transgressions against masculine authority will render her outcast from the community. The lesson to be learned from stories about witches was that a powerful woman will end up ugly, lonely, sexually frustrated and extremely vulnerable to persecution. In the witch craze the Church taught women a 'moral' lesson about the penalties of exercising female power and intellectual, religious and sexual independence. When patriarchal scholars and religionists narrate the story of the witch craze (usually with some relish), women and girls continue to be taught that lesson.

However, feminist witchcraft gives a very different account of itself; one that will be best understood in the context of a brief exposition of Wicca as a whole and as it has been practised since the late 1940s (see Crowley 1995: 81-93). Contemporary witchcraft (or Wicca, the Old Religion, the Craft, as it is variously called) can be understood as a revival of 'the ancient shamanic religion of the West and Middle East' (Roney-Dougal 1991: 211), or, more generally, as a Pagan earth-based mystery religion which reverences the European pre-Christian deities. Wicca is not a cult; it is without any charismatic leader or central organization. There is no sacred text whose authority is comparable to the Jewish and Christian Bible. Mainstream Wicca is plural and acknowledges feminist and Dianic Wicca (an especially gynocentric, sometimes lesbian separatist, form of Wicca) as part of the Wiccan tradition.

Wicca is Goddess–centred and practised by both men and women. Its deities are the Goddess or Great Mother and her consort the Horned God who is part human and part animal.[1] These may be some of the world's most ancient deities. Arguably, however, Wicca is not ditheistic. Most Wiccans understand the Goddess and the God as a sexual duality within the one divine reality. (It is only Dianic Wiccans who see the ultimate divinity as female in character—the God being relegated to her

---

1.   The Horned God must not be confused with the devil who is a later Christian sub-deity. The Horned God is the pre-Christian god of, among other things, horned beasts, shepherds, hunting and farming (Roney-Dougal 1991: 210-11).

child with no significant role of his own). The Wiccan divine is not entirely without transcendence, but is primarily immanent in nature. This means that the material world is a manifestation of divine energy; there is no division between matter and spirit so that, unlike the world-denying, puritanical forms of Christianity, all things, including the human body and human sexuality are sacred. Wicca is not at all an ascetic tradition; although promiscuity is not encouraged, sexual desire is a sacred power, not a mark of spiritual failure and alienation from God.

Time takes a circular rather linear form in Wicca. The Goddess and the God are worshipped through the cycle of eight festivals (sabbats) and the thirteen full moons (esbats). Accordingly, there is no concept of a final salvation or damnation. Without any sense of the original or innate sinfulness of humanity, Wiccan morality is largely self-regulating, though ever vigilant against causing harm to others. The Wiccan 'congregations' consist of covens—relatively small, autonomous groups of people who meet outdoors or in each other's homes. Many Wiccans, however, prefer to practice alone as Wise Women or Cunning Men through private magical practice and communion with nature (Beth 1990; Green 1991). Wiccans do not proselytize or initiate minors and try to ensure that people seeking to join a coven are not attempting to gain power over others through magic or to exploit others sexually. Wicca is practised in varying degrees of secrecy, though this is not merely self-dramatizing. Ill-informed prejudice against Paganism is such that Wicca is often erroneously confused with Satanism (a Christian heresy) and known witches may run the risk of losing a job or being considered unfit to be a parent to their child.[2]

---

2.   As Pagans are compelled to repeat, Satanism is a perversion of Christianity, probably no older than 150 years. Elements of Wicca certainly predate the invention of Satanism and, arguably, can be traced back to ancient Egyptian magical practices. However, Satanism, whose very existence is hotly debated by psychologists, social workers and social scientists is a 'black' or reversed form of the Catholic Mass and Satanists worship the devil. Pagans and others believe this distasteful phenomenon to be a fantasy of Christian anti-Pagan propagandists. In addition, feminist witches utterly repudiate any suggestion that their occultism is linked to the present neo-Nazi revival in Europe and the United States. As Starhawk points out, the Nazi *Übermensch* was a wholly patriarchal construct, as was the highly conservative Nazi ideology of femininity. For all Wiccans, 'differences in color, race, and customs are welcomed as signs of the myriad beauty of the Goddess. To equate Witches with Nazis because neither are Judeo-Christians and both share magical elements is like

The basic ritual sequence for all covens—including feminist ones—is held more or less in common. The practice of Dianic Wicca, for example, usually involves the following sequence of actions. First a circle is cast and consecrated and those entering the circle are purified. The circle is closed and the four directions or corners of the universe are invoked. Witch power is raised. The Goddess is invoked, the magical tools, food and coven members are blessed, and then a ritual specific to the season or the needs of the group (the two types of ritual are not mutually exclusive) takes place. Sometimes the Goddess is channelled or mediated through the facilitating priestess and members of the coven may ask questions of the Goddess. The questions are answered by the priestess as prophet of the Goddess. As in other types of Wicca, this is followed by feasting and dancing and a dismissal of the guardian spirits (Budapest 1986: 17). Wiccan rituals tend to be playful and spontaneous to a degree rarely found among the world's religions.

Unlike most other of the world's religions, in Wicca, men are not privileged over women. Non-Dianic Wiccans perceive themselves as sexually egalitarian and urge male Wiccans to come to understand and value the 'feminine' side of their personalities and vice versa for women. Not all feminist Wiccans would agree that mainstream Wicca is non-sexist, but it is undeniable that female divinity figures far more prominently in Wicca than it does in the Abrahamic traditions: 'Witchcraft is the only Western religion that recognizes woman as a divinity in her own right' (Goldenberg 1979: 98). Indeed, the 'feminine' and female sexuality is necessary to the practice and meaning of Wicca. The priestess and priest are particularly experienced witches who lead the ritual as representatives of the Goddess and the God. As a pair, they channel and direct the energy of the coven and represent a life-giving unity and balance: a 'sacred marriage' of nature's masculine and feminine elements. For Wiccans, the transcendent masculinity of the Judaeo-Christian God has a deathly character in that it is severed from the feminine life principle. In Wicca, the divine is imaged as a generative balance of masculine and feminine elements with, in practice, more emphasis being placed on the Goddess/feminine principle than the God/masculine principle as the former is primarily the giver of life.

saying that swans are really scorpions because neither are horses and both have tails' (Starhawk 1982: 56. See also, Göttner-Abendroth 1991: 221-23).

Above all, Wicca is a mystery religion. This means that it uses rites of initiation to effect permanent psycho-spiritual transformation and, ultimately, union with the divine. Through three degrees of initiation and Wiccan study and practice the initiate comes to alter their sense of self. The ego and self-image of everyday consciousness is gradually replaced by a knowledge of the true, divine Self which encompasses but also transcends the ego and is the source of energy, vision and creativity.

The Feminist Reclamation of Witchcraft

What is complex about feminist witchcraft is that it reclaims the witch from popular demonology, but not all the qualities of the patriarchal witch have been entirely repudiated. For without inspiring a degree of numinous awe and without having the power to change reality to the detriment of patriarchal interests, a feminist witch would simply not be a witch.

The word 'witch' is, as Rudolf Otto would say, *unheimlich*: an untranslatable word roughly meaning odd, eerie, strange, and with qualities that awaken the *sensus numinis*—the sense of the Otherness of the sacred which lies beyond ordinary moral or rational categories of understanding. The fear and veneration sacred things or people evoke are continuous numinous emotions. If the word 'witch' ceased to evoke a degree of religious awe or fear (that is, a numinous reaction) it would have forfeited its sacrality. The Otherness of the witch's title is a part of her power—it is a sign that her energies cannot be assimilated into and diffused by patriarchal structures of exploitation.

Although feminsts of all types want to overcome our culture's fear or distrust of female power, feminist witches may also want to retain the title 'witch' as it connotes that female religion is not only constituted by feminine compassion and nurturing. For Budapest, 'witch' means priestess; it is the 'only word in English that denotes "woman with spiritual power"' (1986: xvii). Starhawk describes herself and others like her as 'witches' because the word 'witch' forces people to confront the reasons *why* they fear the word. Moreover, the word 'witch' 'reeks of holy stubbornness' (Starhawk 1987: 8); it demonstrates the integrity of feminists in the commitment to beliefs that might well leave them socially ostracised. In this sense, feminist witches declare their solidarity with the persecuted witches of the past.

The use of the term 'witch' does not, however, necessarily imply that feminist witchcraft is identical or even strictly continuous with ancient or mediaeval witchcraft. Although most feminist witches perceive themselves as at least participant in an ancient global tradition of wise women, there is also a widespread view that, as Naomi Goldenberg puts it, 'scholarly arguments about the history of witchcraft have obscured serious study of the modern phenomenon. Whatever one decides about witches of the past, it is witches of the present who are building a powerful religion (Goldenberg 1979: 90).[3]

Nonetheless, feminist witches are well aware that the word 'witch' is far from respectable. Witches have been, and remain, the outcasts of the Western religious community. Like the word 'heretic', 'witch' summons sinister images of one who slowly and secretly unpicks the fabric of civilization. Of feminist witches, this image would not be entirely wide of the mark: they would certainly want to say that bringing about the end of patriarchy would involve, among other things, a magical exercise of directed will and consciousness. The words of 1 Sam. 15.23, 'Rebellion is as the sin of witchcraft' can be read as patriarchy itself suggesting witchcraft's potential as an instrument of political subversion. In Dianic Wiccan tradition, Aradia, the daughter of the goddess Diana and the only known female avatar or deity to appear in human female form, was sent to liberate humanity from oppression. When she rejoined Diana she left spells so that she could be conjured to come to women's assistance in the present political struggle (Budapest 1986: 23).

While patriarchy's tales of witches are an attempt to make rebellious women afraid of what they could turn into and what could be done to them, the feminist witch is a warning to patriarchy that female sacral power represents energies stronger and older than patriarchy; 'women can call down nature in their own behalf' (Budapest 1986: 17). And let loose, these powers of resistance can introduce chaotic disequilibrium into all the social institutions and stratifications of patriarchy. That patriarchy fears this is demonstrated by its very demonization of empowered women, a contemporary example of which is that of the far-right Christian evangelical, the Reverend Pat Robertson who preaches that the Equal Rights Amendment would encourage women to 'leave their

3. An exceptionally useful film account of contemporary feminist witchcraft and its heritage is Donna Read's *The Burning Times*, National Film Board of Canada, 1990.

husbands, kill their children, practice witchcraft, destroy capitalism, and become lesbians'.[4]

Witchcraft is traditionally accused by Christians of reversing and perverting the order of nature and allying itself with evil powers (Douglas 1973: 138; Durkheim 1971: 44). In fact, although feminist witchcraft intends the dissolution of patriarchy as an institution, it intends precisely the opposite of evil, but rather seeks to restore nature's own order and allies itself with all struggles for justice. Feminist witches make a strenuous attempt to repair and strengthen the web of life and not to exploit the earth, but to leave it as they find it (Brooke 1993: 7, 138). This implies that it is patriarchal warfare, colonialism and capitalism, not women, which are guilty of the crimes of chaos and destruction patriarchy calls witchcraft.

It must be stressed, then, that all feminist witches refuse the association of female witchcraft and evil. On the contrary, feminist Wiccans perceive themselves as practitioners of an ancient European rural religion inherited from pre-Christian matrifocal Old Religion which was stamped out during the witch craze (see Murray 1931, 1921). One of the central features of the Old Religion was that of healing. Barbara Ehrenreich and Deirdre English's interpretation of the witch craze as the elimination of unlicensed village midwife-healers or wise women by their male competitors in the new medical profession finds widespread support in the spiritual feminist community (1972). Starhawk has also offered an account of the roots of the witch craze (much of which could be found in standard secular historiography of the witch craze). According to Starhawk, the persecution of (mainly) peasant women as witches can be attributed not only to the perception of female powers as evil, but also to the social and ideological upheaval of the sixteenth and seventeenth centuries. The witch-hunts were, she argues, 'linked to three interwoven processes: the expropriation of land and natural resources, the expropriation of knowledge; and the war against the consciousness of immanence which was embodied in women, sexuality and magic' (Starhawk 1990a: 189).

It should be noted that the politics of the feminist reclamation of witchcraft also entails rejecting any claim some of its other practitioners might make to its exclusive, esoteric status. Although feminist covens usually counsel discretion (at least) on the part of their members, the

---

4.   Roundtable discussion on 'Backlash', *Journal of Feminist Studies in Religion* 10 (1994): 91, 107.

political intentions of feminist Wicca prohibit the kind of secrecy that other Wiccans usually prefer to adopt. The very point of feminist Wicca is to awaken every woman's sense of her own power and of the connection between the exercise of the private will and collective political transformation. Spiritual feminism's most famous coven, Zsuzsanna Budapest's Susan B. Anthony Coven No. 1 began as an experiment with a 'handful' of women on the Winter Solstice of 1971, and expanded into a coven of up to 120 women.[5] Budapest and many feminists like her discarded traditional Wiccan oaths of secrecy on the grounds that they could not teach the new and growing women's religion under those conditions (Spretnak 1982: 535). They also broke with tradition by limiting the coven circles to women only and only working with men in workshops on the 'men's mysteries' (Budapest 1986: xi).

Feminist witchcraft encourages women to take what responsibility they can for their own lives and not to see themselves as victims alone, but it does not demand extraordinary spiritual or intellectual gifts on the part of its practitioners. Although feminist Wicca does require a degree of skill, concentration, study and self-discipline, there are no compulsory rites of initiation to be endured or esoteric texts to be fathomed. There are no hierarchies to obey or to subject others to judgment. There are no binding ties to the coven. Nor need feminist Wiccans separate themselves from the heterosexual community if they do not wish to do so, and most feminist covens model themselves on Starhawk's more sexually integrated approach. Lesbian witches, however, might feel especially comfortable in Dianic covens as these can be separatist. According to Shân Jayran, a Dianic 'dedicates herself to the Goddess exclusively, and to women's mysteries . . . While few would want to dedicate themselves as Dianics for life, most women [witches] need or want recourse to women's mysteries at some time in their lives' (1985: 35).

Wicca is also unusually self-expressive among the world's religions. Not only can women create their own rituals, dances and chants, they can also sacralize their own space by designing an altar in one or more rooms in their homes. An altar is usually assembled on a table or similar

5.   Budapest's coven is named after the nineteenth-century Quaker suffragist Susan B. Anthony. She is invoked as guardian spirit of the coven because she promised that 'When I die I shall go neither to heaven nor to hell, but stay right here and finish the women's revolution' (Budapest 1986: xviii).

surface according to individual tastes and needs. Goddess figurines, flow-
ers, shells and other natural objects, small objects of personal significance, mirrors, ritual tools, candles, salt for purification and so forth can
be placed upon the altar. The altar can change its form and contents
depending on the woman's mood and needs and the season. As such,
these altars 'are frequently a medium of self-representation. The altar is
the self, symbolized and idealized and set in right relation with the
world' (Eller 1993: 107-108).

The whole world view of the witch runs counter to the Western
patriarchal religious and philosophical tradition. As Naomi Goldenberg
discusses, for witches, as for psychoanalysts,

> the inner world of anticipation and wish is the basis for all human thought
> and action. Consciousness and directed rational thought are considered to
> be relatively superficial phenomena which derive from older, more en-
> compassing unconscious structures (Goldenberg 1995: 157).

Nonetheless, this does not make feminist Wicca an occult metaphysic
for the illuminati. Thealogy brings masculinist metaphysical gods, duties
and values down to ('female') earth, grounding them in embodied life
and (in the widest sense) erotic desire.

In Starhawk's words, 'witchcraft has always been a religion of poetry,
not theology. The myths, legends, and teachings are recognized as metaphors for "That-Which-Cannot-Be-Told"' (Spretnak 1982: 49). In
other words, the Wiccan mysteries are participant experiences whose
meaning is essentially non-rational and cannot be conveyed by description and analysis alone. For this reason I have tried in the present
chapter to give feminist witches their own voice as far as possible. But
witches themselves find language an inadequate medium for experiences
that are better poetically evoked than described. As the traditional *Charge
of the Goddess* goes,

> And thou who thinkest to seek for me,
> know thy seeking and yearning shall avail thee not,
> unless thou knowest the mystery;
> that if that which thou seekest thou findest not within thee,
> thou wilt never find it without thee.
> For behold, I have been with thee from the beginning
> and I am that which is attained at the end of desire
> (*Pagan Federation* 1993: 9).

So talk of Wiccan thealogy and the magical will should not convey the
impression that feminist Wicca is a primarily cerebral religion. This is

not the case. De-Anna Alba emphasizes that, whether alone or in a coven, power is raised not just through the mind/imagination but also from the solar plexus, or as she prefers, from the womb: 'the source of female creativity. It is where babies take root and grow. It is the seat of one of the greatest creative processes in the natural world.' When raising and releasing power in the circle, Alba adopts an upright birthing position, pushing out the power from her body as if she were giving birth to a baby (Alba 1993: 60; see also Stein 1993: 121).

Feminist magical power flows with the lunar/biological cycle:

> The bleeding time, no matter when it occurs in the Lunar cycle, is a particularly powerful time for women. Psychic abilities are usually strongest during the menstrual cycle, and many women feel a need to turn inward, to be alone, to seek personal visions, to contact the inner plane (Otherworld) . . . (Alba 1993: 46).

Chanting, drumming and dancing are also ways of opening and focusing consciousness so as to direct and release its magical flow around and through the body, the group and the cosmos. Alba writes, 'For me [Dianic Wicca] is a form of worship that has had a profound impact on my life. I let go and let the Goddess sing me, and I feel a connection with Her that I am unable to duplicate in other ways' (1993: 56).

The Use of Magic in Feminist Wicca

Spiritual feminists are commonly sympathetic to the use of a variety of healing and divination techniques. These include the *I Ching*, astrology and Tarot readings for divination, and acupuncture and aura reading for healing (see Stein 1993). But as well as these, feminist witches use magic itself. Magic, according to Starhawk (following Dion Fortune), is the art of changing consciousness and therefore reality, by the exercise of will in visualizing, raising and directing healing energy towards its object (Starhawk 1987: 18-19).

Most Westerners' view of magic is, however, rather different, and in order to understand many people's hostility to the idea of feminist witchcraft, it is necessary to understand how magic has been perceived in modern religion and science. In modernity witchcraft has become a symbol of 'primitive' religion unredeemed from the darkness of ignorance. Since the seventeenth century, Protestantism, colonialism and science have all in their different ways contrasted the religious, racial and intellectual purity of modern Europe with that of the Others who

practise witchcraft. Protestant polemics have depicted any kind of ritu-
alism as a dangerous and subversive superstition, and, until recently,
where Protestants have found magic practised by the 'savages' of its
colonies this has been similarly demonized as evidence of the sub-reli-
giosity of the non-white, non-Christian Other (see Smart 1996: 36).

Western modernity has regarded those who practise magic as prim-
itives who merely attempt to manipulate nature's impersonal powers.
Modern, that is, post-Reformation, Christianity is inherently hostile to
the magical world view because its God is alone in control of a creation
that has no intrinsic 'livingness' or consciousness of its own. This Protestant view of nature as inanimate and non-sacral buttressed modern
physics. As scientific discourse gained ascendency, it was held that 'the
unliving world of the sun, the moon, lightening and fires could be
explored better through physical (dead) principles. Physics joined forces
with Western monotheism to banish the gods' (Smart 1996: 37).[6] And
Christianity has not only viewed magicians as sunk in pre-modern error;
they are also considered immoral, setting themselves 'above' God's holy
will and bending it to their own. Christians, by contrast, claim to have
an obedient personal relationship with a real, personal God who is
worshipped for his own sake alone.[7]

Although the earliest historians of religion perpetuated Christian
prejudices against non-Christian (especially non-literate) religions, more
recent historians of religion recognize that labelling a phenomenon
'religion' rather than 'magic' is an ideological and dogmatic evaluation
more than it is a strictly scientific distinction. In practice the two cannot
always be clearly differentiated. Moreover, a strict distinction between
magico-religious thinking and scientific thinking is becoming equally
difficult to maintain. Twentieth-century anthropology has demonstrated
'the logical character and theoretical sophistication' of the so-called 'sav-
age mind' and recent philosophers of science such as Michael Polanyi
and Thomas Kuhn have shown science to be providing less objective
truths about reality than scientists had previously supposed (Eilberg-

    6.   See also Pahnke (1995: 165-67). This paper offers an important analysis of
thealogy's transformation of the concept of magic and the implications of that for
the contemporary study of religion.
    7.   The Bible prohibits witchcraft (Exod. 22:18: 'You shall not permit a sor-
ceress to live'). The story in 1 Sam. 28 in which Saul consults the witch of Endor
shows that Israel did not tolerate wizards and necromancers and had sent them 'out
of the land'. See Walker (1988: 142).

Schwartz 1989: 86-87). A number of influential modern physicists are now taking a far less materialistic, atomistic approach to their subject than was previously the case, and even draw on mystical discourse in the exposition of theory (Roney-Dougal 1991: 65-89; 229-47). Furthermore, the magical world view is far from absent from the biblical religions and especially their esoteric traditions. (Accounts of Jesus' miracles in the Gospels, the *acta* of the Catholic saints, and certain forms of petitionary prayer have clearly magical elements.)

The persistence of the nineteenth-century distinction between religion and magic is significant in that feminists who remain within the biblical traditions might regard feminist witchcraft as merely a self-interested and therefore sub-religious set of practices. This is not (or only rarely) the case. As we have seen, traditional distinctions between magic and religion focus on magic as a service to a paying clientele and as mere *technique*—a method of using personal and cosmic power to bend reality to the private purposes of the human will. But in the case of feminist witchcraft, this distinction between religion and magic cannot be upheld on two counts at least. First, feminist magic is not traded for money. Priestesses are not accustomed to take money for facilitating rituals in the coven and they do not perform spells on other women's behalf—whether for money or for free. Feminist magic is about women's *self-empowerment* and therefore women must develop a magical will of their own (See Weinstein 1978; 1986; Brooke 1993: 152-69). (Sales of books, Tarot readings, lectures, workshops and so forth can, however, be a legitimate source of earnings [Budapest 1982: 539; Alba 1993: 24-25].)

Second, and more importantly, the feminist thealogy of magic is distinct from that of other witches—some of whose use of magic could accurately be described as hubristic. By absolute contrast with many non-feminist magicians, the political and theological emphases of feminist Wiccans lend their concept of magic a degree of non-coercive relationality not found elsewhere. As Susan Greenwood has made clear, the feminist theory of magic is best understood by comparison with a paradigmatically patriarchal theory: that of Aleister Crowley's Thelemic magic. Crowley understood the masculine magical will in a Nietzschean sense as the will to power, exercise of which released the individual magician from the petty bonds of altruism and humanitarianism into a realm of absolute freedom (Greenwood 1995: 191-203).

Feminist witchcraft is quite different: it is concerned with finding the power of the self in and through its ontological connection with all living things. That ecological quality of feminist magic is more significant than whether a spell always 'works' in the sense of making an immediate, visible difference.[8] While feminist witches would accept Shân Jayran's general definition of a witch as 'a woman or a man who has trained in the use of their own natural powers' (1985: 5), a feminist witch is above all concerned to use those powers to empower her work in a political struggle whose character is that of social, ecological, psychological and bodily healing. Feminist magical thinking does not take charge of the sacred in the sense that a patriarchal 'high' magician or magus seeks to stand above nature by harnessing its power to his private ends. Indeed, feminists who use magic are not properly called 'magicians', as the latter usually connotes a masculinist intellectual endeavour that may have little or no religious content (Jayran 1985: 49).

Feminist witches by no means consider themselves 'above' the Goddess as traditional theories of magic might imply. In the coven setting, the role of High Priestess rotates around the coven members and decision-making and discussions about the meaning of the ritual are (sometimes laboriously), democratic (see Luhrmann 1994: 55-56). Rotating the role of priestess ensures that she is not endowed with charismatic power that might be wielded over the rest (Adler 1986: 220-21). Within the sacred circle the facilitating priestess may begin a ritual by channelling or 'aspecting' the Goddess into and through herself in a ritual known as 'Drawing Down the Moon'. This is a prophetic act, in which the facilitating priestess 'draw[s] the essence of the Goddess into her consciousness' and can, in that state, 'speak' the Goddess for the good of the whole group (Alba 1993: 115-16). But again, this prophetic function does not lend her even temporary power over the rest, for they are themselves priestess and Goddess in so far as they are Goddess women, ritual practitioners and sources of wisdom to those who ask for their guidance (Jayran 1985: 54).

---

8.   Pam Lunn argues that if spells and rituals do not make a real change in 'the real external world' then they might be merely 'an emotional opiate, a consolation prize' (1993: 17-38). Certainly, any religion can degenerate into the latter, but feminist witches, in common with others of a postmodern frame of mind, would question whether the 'the real external world' is an objective reality whose existence transcends (the very political nature of) its naming.

Although feminist witchcraft does not place the desires of the individual over the collective good, it values idiosyncrasy. There are no compulsory elements in a given ritual; and most feminist witches either customize rituals from books by witches like Starhawk, Brooke or Budapest, or devise them themselves. This degree of spontaneity and participation within the feminist coven is not generally found in mainstream Wicca (Luhrmann 1994: 56).[9] For this reason some Wiccans regard feminist witchcraft as something of a short cut to the achievement of power-from-within. The feminist claim that any woman who has reclaimed her own power is thereby a witch is not, according to Shân Jayran, the former Dianic (and now Shamanic) priestess and witch, 'a contradiction to the Wiccan tradition, but it stops short of the lengthy structured training usually undertaken by initiates of the tradition' (1985: 4).

For feminist witches, the stipulations and style of the Wiccan tradition may be of less importance than the newer traditions of feminist spirituality and thealogy. Indeed, the spiritual feminist practice of magic is quite distinct from patriarchal (high) magic in that for the former, 'magic is no longer an expression of an irrational–omnipotent attitude of human power *over* nature and the supernatural, but rather an expression of solidarity and inclusiveness *within* nature and the supernatural'. Magic is, for all spiritual feminists, a means of (re)establishing the channels of energy that flow through life itself in all its connected dimensions: human, natural and cosmic (Pahnke 1995: 170-71). Whereas a magician like Crowley was not concerned with the good of the social and planetary whole, but with the fulfilment of the individual, feminists' ultimate purpose in using magic is to transform patriarchy into the kind of holistic, egalitarian democracy that is already manifest in their own non-hierarchical religion (Greenwood 1995: 193-97). Feminist witchcraft repudiates any magical exercise of 'power-over' others or the violation of another's will. For it is patriarchal power-over others that precisely alienates and obstructs the life-giving energy (equivalent to what the Chinese call *chi*) that spiritual feminism seeks to liberate.

De-Anna Alba, a Dianic witch, offers a succinct account of the thealogical cosmology that underpins spiritual feminism's use of magic.

---

9.   Tanice Folz and Wendy Griffin offer important ethnographic insights into the ritual practices of an American feminist coven (1996: 301-29). What is also interesting about this paper is its authors' account of the transformations the process of researching a feminist coven wrought in themselves.

Alba writes that imagination, 'in concert with the vast pool of creative energy available in the universe' can be drawn upon for any creative labour and may be called Goddess energy/power.

> Witches believe this power comes from the Goddess, that it is a part of Her essence. Since we are also a part of her essence and partake in small measure of Her divinity, this creative or Magickal energy/power is inherent within us as well. This is referred to as personal power. We make Magick by accessing this power within and combining it with the power available in the universe. With it, we can transform our lives and the world (Alba 1986: 35).

Magical thinking is more, then, than just positive thinking, although that can have a real effect on people's self-confidence and therefore their ability to cope with and change their circumstances. Feminist witchcraft values the will in its capacity to direct consciousness towards change, but for feminists that magical will is always biophilic and tempered by its need to harmonize the collective consciousness and energy of the coven with nature, both of whose energies have endowed the witch with her power in the first place. The spiritual feminist assumption that nature is ultimately cooperative and life-seeking, and that energy is generated in webs or networks, means that malign magic is neither meaningful nor effective.

That said, feminist witchcraft may also use magic to benefit the self (though not at the expense of others). Spells for getting jobs and improving one's finances, recovering from illness, finding lost objects, and protecting one's home and loved ones are readily available in feminist Wiccan manuals (see, e.g., Brooke 1993: 144-46). Diane Stein, for example, describes how Gloria, then a homeless woman, successfully worked a candle spell to draw money to her and her daughter. She bought a large candle from a second-hand shop for 50 cents and carved one of Marion Weinstein's magical rhymes on its side: 'Money, money, come to me / money come right away / as I will, so mote it be.' Making clear to herself that this spell should not be the cause of anyone else's deprivation, she visualized counting out the money for necessities and the pleasure the money would bring to her daughter and others, while the candle burnt beside her for two nights. Within days she found work and a bag of money that was never claimed. She then lit the candle again to give thanks and to assure the Goddess that this was sufficient (Stein 1993: 129-31). To this extent, a measure of self-interest can become enmeshed with the more altruistic political and ecological purposes of spell-craft, though as is evident from Gloria's story, it need not contradict them. Those who have studied Christian and Jewish theology may find it difficult to see this kind of spell-craft as religious, though in popular religious devotion people have always petitioned the divine for things that they want or need.

Diane Stein clearly experiences no conflict between her work for the peace, women's and gay rights movements and also catering to her personal needs through magic. For her, the Goddess is a plenitude offering an abundance of good things which an equitable social system, as well as women who are confident enough to exercise their wills, will make available to all. Like all witches, Stein urges women to 'be careful what you ask for, you may get it'. But for her, patriarchy's 'best kept secret' is that women have actually got the power to get what they want. 'Greed isn't necessary, there is abundance in the Goddess universe for all, enough for everyone without anyone being deprived or hurt' (Stein 1993: 132, 120, 139). After a mystical experience in which Stein felt herself turn into a tree taking nourishment from the earth and sky, she came to the realisation: 'If I need something, it is there. It has been there all along' (1993: 120).

Thealogians regard the beneficence of feminist witchcraft as simply self-evident. Although Wiccan ethics are realistic rather than idealistic, feminist witches are acutely aware of their ethical responsibilities when using magic. The natural power magic directs is itself ethically neutral, but human intentions are not, therefore feminist witches are vigilant in guarding against their magic causing harm. 'Love for life is the basic ethic of Witchcraft. Witches are bound to honour and respect all living things, and to serve the life force' (Starhawk 1982b: 53). Feminist witches believe that magic must not be abused by using it to abuse others. This refusal to interfere with the exercise of another's free will usually rules out positive magic as well. Casting love spells or spells to heal another without their being aware of it not encouraged: 'To invade someone's body or mind with Magickal energy of any kind is an act of negative Magick' (Brooke 1993; Alba 1993).

All spiritual feminists recognise the dangers of hexing (cursing), blasting (psychic attack) and binding (ways of curtailing another's chosen course of action). And the majority of feminist witches believe that hexing and blasting must never be used to carry out personal vendettas. The vast majority of 'positive practitioners', including Starhawk, feel that hexing is a dangerous practice that produces bad karmic effects (see

Eller 1993: 124-29). Elisabeth Brooke recommends that if a person has been harmed by another, instead of using a hex, that negative energy should be merely sent back to him or her and, using meditation techniques, all connections with that person should be broken (1993: 137). Negative magic worked upon the innocent (and even the guilty) can rebound threefold on its sender and binding violates its object's freedom of will.

However, a very small minority of feminist witches feel that hexing can be used in self-defence. Zsuzsanna Budapest and Luisah Teish are two influential feminist witches who feel justified in retaliating against rapists and other attackers known to be guilty. Budapest and Teish do not believe the (justifiably) negative energies of their anger will rebound on them. Hexing or binding is not only a form of justice, it will stop a rapist in his tracks and therefore benefits the whole community (see Eller 1993: 123-29). Budapest instructs her readers in the making of hexes and the preparation of a black altar; for her, the power to hex is the obverse side of the sacred power to heal, and so 'a witch who cannot hex cannot heal' (1986: 43). After twice being moved out of their covenstead in Malibu, Budapest (the coven's High Priestess), unrepentantly ignoring standard Wiccan advice against casting spells in anger, reported, 'I angrily stomped my foot, pointed to the house which had twice called the police on us and said, "The third time YOU GO!" (this place today is known as the Great Malibu Land-slide)' (1982: 539).

But even for these 'Aradian' witches, hexing is not merely malevolent. It is a response to an evil act that has already taken place and which has a victim. It is also an attempt to limit the course of that evil act by incapacitating the person committing it. The innocent must never be attacked and, in any case, the Goddess can 'veto' a spell. For all witches, the 'only law of the Goddess is love' and where the Goddess destroys she only does so to create new life, not to oppress or destroy for her own sake (Alba 1993: 23-24). Accordingly, it would be acceptable for witches to 'wish' for the non-violent, 'natural' end of patriarchy. This would not be negative magic as the hex would result in a new political dispensation and one that would renew the flow of love and life on the earth. Nonetheless, it may be fair to say that the philosophical problem of how one exercises power through magic entirely without harm or coercion is rarely adequately addressed.

To conclude, there is little doubt that feminist witchcraft can offer post-Christian feminists religious practices that are politically engaged *and* which profoundly honour female embodiment. Wicca has a female object of celebration, mediated through the self and through a like-minded and supportive coven. The transformatory power of the Goddess cannot be detached from that of a woman's own wise, resistant female self. If the Old English word *wicce* and its stem, *wic*, connote not only a wise woman, but also the skill of bending and weaving (as in the craft of wickerwork) (Goldenberg 1979: 96), this suggests that the Wiccan Self is one who is skilled in the practical as well as theoretical craft of revisioning and reconstructing what we experience as real and of value. In other words, the feminist witch is a paradigm shifter. 'Witch' then comes to name an ontological and existential choice, defining a woman as a magical activist.

This witch self is also experienced as rooted in a female line, perhaps running through a family from mother to daughter or through a tradition of wise women whose origin is lost in the mists of time. A feminist witch has a sense of participating in a history or heritage which gives her opportunities and techniques for spiritual leadership, self-empowerment and protection that at the same time empower and protect nature itself. These are no minzr attractions for women more used to religious marginality or spectator status. Tanice Folz and Wendy Griffin usefully summarize what they perceive to be of particular value about feminist witchcraft:

> We believe the unique power of feminist Witchcraft lies in (1) the transformative potential of its innovative rituals, (2) the tactic experience of immanence through body-prayer, (3) the promise of integration of self and mind with the female body, (4) integration of the self with a spiritual community, and (5) its vision of a truly humane, peaceful, and ecologically sane world (1996: 325).

We have seen that feminist witchcraft preserves the numinosity of its craft, while at the same time resisting its demonization and offering it as a morally and politically credible religious option. This strategy of demystifying witchcraft may also have made a substantial contribution to the reconciliation of white Anglo-Saxon society with the anti-typical Others such as Jews and Blacks who, to varying degrees, inhabit its margins. As Howard Eilberg-Schwartz has written of contemporary American witchcraft:

The witch is no longer an 'other' that helps by way of negation to define who we are. Nor is the witch an entity against whom we can and must collectively unite. On the contrary, witches are now recognizable and respectable members of our society with whom we share a great many common interests and values (1989: 84).

Chapter Seven

Thealogy: Concluding Reflections on the Debate

In this conclusion I want to summarize and reflect briefly upon the central themes and evaluative commentary I have presented in the six previous chapters of this book, not so as to exhaust debate but rather to invite further reflection on the part of the reader. To begin with, it might be useful to rehearse some of the most serious and the most recurrent criticisms that have been levelled at thealogy, and then, finally, to suggest how thealogians could and do respond to this critique.

Taking Issue with Thealogy

It is quite clear that the theological project does not entirely win the support of all religious feminists—especially reformist religious feminists. Some feminists might argue that I have made too rigid (and old fashioned) a distinction between radical and reformist feminism. I have, throughout this book, indicated the continuities between them, but it does seem to me that Goddess feminism in particular represents a group of issues and strategies that really *do* divide feminists rather sharply. Reformist feminism generally assumes modern notions of rational/moral progress and human perfectibility and seeks a liberated future through legal and religious reform and negotiation. Reformists are suspicious of any appeal to the pre-modern (let alone the prehistoric) to achieve liberation. Wishing to demystify women—to liberate women from patriarchal religion's tendency to cast women as angelic mothers or demonic temptresses—the reenchantment of women that characterizes the theological project is rejected from the outset. Once more to cast women *as* nature, is for reformist feminism, to revive the patriarchal denigratory association of femaleness and naturalness; it is merely to reinforce patriarchy's divorce of femaleness and rational/moral intellection.

Reformist feminism, perhaps less optimistic than Goddess feminism that patriarchal ideologies of femininity can be simply 're-meant' in a post-patriarchal context, is always wary of inadvertently reinforcing stereotypes of women as Other to reason and culture.[1]

So too, thealogy's more secular feminist critics are not persuaded by spiritual feminism's contention that the spiritual *is* the political and are concerned that thealogy's tendency to render political empowerment as a psychological/spiritual process is to privatize the dynamics of political change to the detriment of effective protest in the 'real world' of the public domain. Thealogy can be criticized for making too heavy an investment in the hope that political transformation will be consequent upon a critical mass of individuals experiencing psychological transformation and, for witches, the development of their magical will. Although not referring to spiritual feminism as such, Hester Eisenstein stresses that 'the psychological interacts with the economic, the social and political. A feminist analysis that locates power only in individual psychology is both naive and damaging' (1984: 131-32). Although I believe it is simplistic to talk of a 'real' world as if it were a finished, factual object standing over and against that envisioned in spiritual feminist ritual, dream and praxis, there are clearly dangers in thinking that reality is just a matter of how you think about it or want it to be. It is arguable that structures of military power and economic exploitation are real (all too real) and cannot be *only* wished away.

Other political questions have also dominated the debate over thealogy. Popular thealogy has exposed itself to criticism for failing to attend to academic discussions about essentialism, ethnocentrism and the uncritical use of the category 'women's experience' (as is true of most popular religious thought). Pam Lunn has criticized the Goddess movement for being predominantly populated by white middle class women universalizing their values and experience as if they were those of their sisters around the globe and for thealogizing in ways oblivious to historicity (1993: 21). Thealogical discourse is marked by what Lunn calls 'magpie-like eclecticism' and 'often uncritical syncretism' (1993: 24) and has placed insufficient emphasis upon difference, context and particularity. Motherhood, for example, may not institute the timeless relationships spiritual feminism would have us believe, but can be seen

1.   For a useful thealogical defence against common charges made against Goddess religion (in this case, irrationalism, occultism, links with Nazi mythologies, neobiologism, and apoliticality) see Göttner-Abendroth (1991: 213-29).

as a construction which in its European form is dateable to the rise of Protestantism and the spiritualized household about 400 years ago (Madsen 1994: 484-85).

Wherever feminists find casual talk of 'women's experience' they should be alert to the risk of falsely universalizing white European and North American experience, and therefore simply erasing that of those who are neither. (Even describing a religion or spirituality as 'feminist' can fail to acknowledge the cultural specificity of such a term, ignoring, for example, womanist, *mujerista*, Asian and Asian–American perspectives.) Western thealogians, who have justifiable grievances, are, nonetheless, not always cognizant of their privileges. Globally, few men and even fewer women are given the opportunity to make ethical judgments upon those in power and to publish their views in books, articles and media appearances.

Thealogy can also be guilty of a variety of other generalizations. For example, nature in the North West of the globe presents a quite different (and more tractable) object of experience than, say, that which women in sub-Saharan Africa experience. Goddess women living in relatively temperate countries are usually at a 'safe distance' from nature. They may be more inclined to indulge in romantic valorizations of a Goddess/nature untamed by modernity or to experience numinous awe at the Goddess/nature's terrible sublimity than those who live in areas suffering the extremes of the global weather system. Or again, black women have been stigmatized by Christian colonial racism as non-rationally 'natural' and 'bodily' in ways that white Goddess women have not. A celebration of naturalness and bodilyness may be read and heard quite differently among different ethnic groups. This may give some Goddess women pause for thought as to how they figure and celebrate numinous and political Otherness. So too, in the 'developed' world, and for middle-class women, pregnancy and childbirth will be differently an object of spiritual reflection and celebration. In a prosperous Western context child bearing does not always necessitate the termination of a woman's ambitions and is rarely life-threatening for the mother. Similarly, thealogy's (and also feminist theology's) confident celebration of embodiment has, according to Angela West, issued from mainly young theorists, for whom the body has not yet demonstrated its capacity to fail its owner (West 1995: 6).[2]

---

2.   It seems worth noting that my own celebratory study of female bodily sacrality—*Thealogy and Embodiment* (1996)—was written immediately after having given

Just as seriously, West has accused spiritual feminism of following an ancient (and implicitly violent) religious pattern in which a longing to recapture purity and innocence entails projecting all evil onto one scape-goat (in this case men) (1995: xviii). Feminist theology, and especially in its thealogical manifestation, has, on this view, merely reversed the old myth of the Fall: now it is Christian dualism and its misogynistic fear and hatred of the body that is the original sin and women, in Eve, no longer represent humanity's guilt, but women's original innocence (1995: 3, 65).

West's scepticism about the post-Christian project originates in her experience at Greenham Common. Although often regarded by British radical feminists of a 'romantic' or thealogical bent as an exemplar of women's pacific nature, West's experience at Greenham culminated with tragic irony in an incident which created a profound rift at the peace camp and left one faction labelling the other racist, so betraying the ideal of solidarity between women of all races (1995: 49-50; 56-57). For her, the rhetoric of women's spirituality does not measure up to reality. At Greenham, 'what began as a movement of women loving women and making space for each other ended up with women tearing each other apart in the name of sisterhood'. The symbolism of men on one side of the wire representing destruction and the women on the other side representing peace could not be sustained (1995: 17-18).

A further common observation of thealogy is that it uses words like 'power', 'patriarchy' and 'patriarchal religion' with insufficient care and attention to the diversities within each tradition. More recent feminist study of religion has rejected what it considers to be a monolithic (often radical feminist) view of patriarchy as always and everywhere necro-philic. Feminist scholars of religion no longer regard religious traditions as uniformly and trans-historically oppressive to women. Postmodern interpretative methods have encouraged feminists to negotiate with, subvert and resist the texts and practices of a tradition that is, or can be made to be, their own. The monotheistic traditions are often morally and politically ambiguous with regard to the status and role of women. More significantly, one prophetic element of a religion is often found to stand in judgment over another element; each tradition has its fresh breeze of liberal, humane, inclusivist, self-reforming activity. This means that texts and traditions can be at once oppressive and liberatory of

birth to my daughter in a decidedly non-natural manner requiring several types of medical intervention which continued to cause discomfort for two further years.

women and all subject others. While thealogy has re-read and reclaimed patriarchal traditions and texts about goddesses, post-Christian thinking as a whole can be criticized for being too little willing to accede that biblical religion holds self-critical counter-traditions within itself or that it can be re-visioned (Madsen 1994: 490-92).

This reluctance to carry on engaging with or 'wresting a blessing' from the patriarchal traditions may originate in some Goddess feminists' sense that to acknowledge their ambiguity would be to weaken claims of their inherent oppressiveness, and obscure the moral and political distinction between oppressor and oppressed. For thealogy to be a revelation (of sorts) it must present crossing over to its new religious territory as a necessary existential choice. However, as Angela West warns, walking out on the Church may first, absolve men of their responsibility of reform, and secondly, 'far from being ultimately liberated [post-Christians] are the ones who have been ultimately conned by men into accepting that the church belongs to men' (West 1995: 84).

Most feminist theologians have also yet to be persuaded that, when analyzed, the concept of the Goddess is as helpful to women as thealogians think it is. Here we are on difficult territory because, as has become clear, thealogy is a practical discourse before it is a theoretical one. Goddess feminists are not, for instance, interested in the presentation of philosophical arguments as evidence for or against the existence of the Goddess. Usually thealogical texts devote far more space to ritual and meditation practices than to thealogical discussion for its own sake. This, and thealogy's refusal of neat thealogical resolutions, has exposed thealogical discourse to the criticism that it cannot furnish women with the kind of theoretical resolution that could ground criticism of patriarchal theology or which could usefully be applied to a given issue or situation.

Feminist theologians might well ask what qualities the Goddess has that would make her worthy of reverence and celebration rather than mere acceptance as some kind of personified karmic law or merely ecological, amoral, sub-personal dynamic of change. Whether the Goddess (or thealogians' concepts of her) can offer, hope and consolation in the face of suffering caused by moral evil remains not entirely clear. Although most thealogians insist that the Goddess is ultimately characterized by love, it is not certain what 'love' means in this context. Most thealogians do not expect juridical justice or moral accountability from the Goddess. She is simply not (yet) that kind of divinity. Even though many Jews and Christians who have suffered find that, in the event, divine compassion, intervention and judgment upon sinners are extremely difficult to detect, it is not yet apparent whether Goddess religion can 'compete' with the conviction of God's love, justice and will to reconciliation that is the great moral strength—even sublimity—of biblical monotheism at its liberative best.

Thealogy and New Religio-Political Possibilities

The points I have outlined above list both my own and other commentator's concerns about thealogy and they are not to be dismissed lightly. Yet many of these points were originally formulated in the late 1970s and early 1980s, in the earliest period of Goddess feminism. Now somewhat stale, this criticism is still reiterated by critics and scholars and students of religion as if it were as necessary now as it might have been 20 years ago. Over 15 years has passed since Rosemary Ruether levelled her oft-quoted arguments against thealogy in *Christianity and Crisis* and in *The Christian Century*. Since then, thealogy has diversified. Thealogy is not and never was a monolith, any more than is any other tradition. Some thealogy is more monotheistic than it once was; few thealogians now have a simplistic attitude to the interpretation of historical evidence for Goddess worship. Most are now sensitive to the ways in which, and the points at which, historiography gives way to thealogy. While the category of 'women's experience' may be bandied about less cautiously than it should be, few spiritual feminists in the postmodern environment of contemporary academia can be oblivious to the gulfs of difference that exist between women of different colour, hemisphere, ethnicity, religion and economic standing. And the less popular thealogical texts are usually careful not to affirm women's or the Goddess's connections to nature and maternity at the expense of their connections to culture. Moreover, the growth of feminist phenomenology of religion since the early days of Goddess feminism has now made it evident to most that, globally, the worship of goddesses does not guarantee the social equality of women.

So while acknowledging the lesser or greater truth of some of the criticisms levelled at thealogy (which is intended to win grassroots support, not academic celebrity), let us also read it more generously. Of course, no one should be allowed to get away with poorly formulated or merely destructive religious theory, but perhaps reformist religious feminism (which predominates in the feminist study of religion) should not be too quick to dismiss radical or post-Christian religious feminism. This is particularly true in the academic context. Not only are there evident commonalties between them, Morny Joy is right that the present feminist academy is enjoying an unprecedented level of vibrant conceptual and investigative activity and it is

> appropriate to allow women to try on/out many diverse modes of thinking and expression in their relation to what they consider sacred . . . Premature closure of constructive debate to establish who has the most legitimate basis, the most politically correct stance, or the most conclusive argument is, at this stage, counter-productive (1995: 140-41).

Admittedly, thealogy is not in the political, religious or academic mainstream; perhaps if it was it would cease to be the definitively prophetic, iconoclastic, post-patriarchal phenomenon it intends to be. But it may not be necessary to evaluate thealogy in terms of its quantitative impact alone. Goddess feminism may be quantitatively insignificant among the world's religions, yet its qualitative significance may be far greater. Thealogy describes yet divinity, the earth and the female body are being unified and charged with sacral powers that signal the possibility of a healed, transformed world order. The sense of personal renewal Goddess feminism has brought to many women may be a preview of the liberation of humanity and nature from those who put economic and military power before life itself. It must be a matter of celebration that, perhaps for the first time since the rise of Christendom in the West (and perhaps long before that), women are able to perceive and treat the material world as the locus of a self-generating divine value and power that can be experienced as something indivisible from themselves as women. It is still too early to assess to what extent and in what ways the reverberations of this shift will change the landscape of Western religion and culture.

The political dimensions of the inclusive (or, to some, undifferentiated) category of 'womanspirit' are too readily dismissed. Spiritual feminism's religious faith in the ontological continuities between women, nature and the Goddess are not necessarily false universalizations. A defining characteristic of thealogy is its awareness of ecological diversity—including that of ethnic, geographical and cultural identities. It postulates, after all, a definitively ecological divinity—a Goddess who, as Gaia, requires diversity and difference of all types for her very survival. But as thealogy is primarily and inherently a religious discourse it will also want to postulate the cosmic/collective dimension of womanspirit. Even if, in fact, the concept of a pure, primary, 'womanspirit' experience unmediated by culture is not philosophically persuasive, the *ideal* is, I think, a good one. Like the now somewhat outmoded term 'sisterhood', 'womanspirit' is a term conducive to a vision of the global solidarity of women in the face of the globalization of capitalism and the environmental devastation it wreaks, and in the face of the global phenomenon of increasing religious fanaticism and the sexism that usually accompanies it.

As Sheila Greeve Devaney (among others) has rightly pointed out, to do away with the concept of female nature and women's experience as such, also raises the following crucial questions:

> Are women, in all our historical particularity, so different from one another that we can no longer speak of "women's experience"? Are historical communities so self-enclosed, so incommensurable that we cannot really communicate with one another? Can we appropriate another community's history, symbols, stories or is that always a form of theft? (1995: 21)

Thealogy assumes femaleness as a political and spiritual identity in itself for strategic reasons, that is, as a banner under which to express an ultimate concern: that of the recovery of biophilic ways of being in the world that are founded upon any woman's right to name herself as Goddess; as fully participant in the divinity of life itself. This strategy turns the patriarchal indictment of woman as Other into a poesis of political and spiritual difference. Here femaleness does not stand for all women everywhere but for a deliberately constructed or self-created essence: a quality of being or spirit that cannot be appropriated or reduced and which defines, grounds and enacts a set of political intentions.

Furthermore, although it has become something of a cliché in thealogical apologies for the Goddess, it remains powerfully true that her celebration as Maiden, Mother and Crone—as sacralizing *all* the phases of female embodiment—can be a central factor in helping women to overcome fear and dislike of their bodily changes in shape and texture over time and under particular biological circumstances. While the psychological benefits of Goddess feminism are not in themselves evidence of its religious truth, there is no doubt that the psychotherapeutic nature of thealogy removes many of the customary obstacles to, and distractions from, women's spiritual/political empowerment (such as an unhealthy absorption in the improvement of one's body in accordance with unrealizable patriarchal ideals) (Raphael 1996b: 83-104). In thealogy, embodied experience of sexuality and change—even death—becomes a part of the meaning of divinity and divine power.

Again, because thealogy is committed to femaleness rather than femininity it is unsentimental in its view of women, accepting women's anger and pain and giving it meaning by accommodating it within the many different visages of the Goddess. Goddess talk may not be to everyone's taste, but it *is* a powerful affirmation of the religious meaning of the female reproductive process, women's emotional life and moral and rational agency—none of which can be affirmed when women are the object of religious discourse and not its subject.

It is also very important to bear in mind that the Goddess is not the transcendental origin and end of all meaning, but rather, offers open and undetermined possibilities of meaning. In this, thealogy reminds us of the metaphorical and provisional nature of religious discourse. Thealogical language is perhaps more fluid or plastic than more tradition-bound religious language. Yet to thealogize on the basis of imagination, dreams and reconstructions of the deep past, refusing any claim to its normativity for others, is a risky undertaking. It is an undertaking that cannot call directly upon the spectacle and sublimity of an architectural, musical and artistic heritage such as is available to most of the world's religions. This is not always to thealogy's advantage. It is not easy to talk about the divine without falling back on the categories of political, philosophical and theological thought that have framed four thousand years of patriarchal history. Doubtless thealogy may be more dependent, for example, on the discourses of the Enlightenment and biblical theology that it might care to admit. To write *in spite of these* as thealogians do, is also, precisely, to be led into (and through) their logic. But the crucial difference is that in thealogy women are affirmed as the subject of their own religious experience, no longer the object of male religious, cultural and aesthetic discourse and law.

Judaeo-Christian prejudice against the Goddess movement will not, I hope, stunt the latter's development as a religious, political and intellectual option, or at least as a way of interrupting, relativizing and criticising conservative theological claims (Weaver 1989: 64). It is still too early to assess how successful it can be in that regard. Goddess feminist communities are as yet only very loosely organized and their cultural impact has yet to be fully felt. But as a number of commentators have argued, whether thealogy continues to persuade growing numbers of individual women and men is perhaps less important than thealogy's capacity to dislodge patriarchal theological idols; to question the apparently necessary, 'natural' and timeless association of masculinity and things divine. Whether they are Goddess feminists or not, almost all religious feminists would surely support Carol Christ's claim that, 'as long as Goddess remains unspeakable, female power is not fully expressed'. The Goddess is 'a symbol that points to the rooting of feminism in the nature of being'. It articulates religious feminism's 'intuition that the struggle for equal rights is supported by the nature of reality' (1987: 156-58).

In the summers between 1981 and 1986, Carol Christ performed rituals at the ruined temple of Eleusis, the site where, in ancient Greece, the agricultural goddesses Demeter and her daughter Persephone had been honoured for about two thousand years. On one of these occasions, described as among the most powerful experiences of her life, Christ, feeling a sense of great loss, reflected upon 'how different our world might have been if we had known a religion that celebrated womanhood and our bonds with our mothers, our daughters' (1987: 200). Perhaps contemporary thealogy can go some way to making good that loss by offering history another chance for such celebration. For thealogy invites a sense that the world might be other than it is; or more, that the world and its divinities 'is' not any one thing but a shifting configuration of possibilities into which thealogy can introduce a new and transformative spiritual–political patterning.

3.   Grigg makes this point of religious feminist communities without particular reference to Goddess feminism (1995: 101).

Bibliography

Adler, M.
    1986   *Drawing Down the Moon: Witches, Druids, Goddess-Worshippers, and Other Pagans in America Today* (Boston: Beacon Press, 2nd edn).

Alba, D.
    1993   *The Cauldron of Change: Myths, Mysteries and Magick of the Goddess* (Oak Park, IL: Delphi Press).

Albatross
    1993   'Declaring the End of Patriarchy', *From the Flames* 11: 13-14.

Albright, M.
    1980   'Ruether: Is She the Organized Enemy?', *WomanSpirit* 7: 48-49.

Amberston, C.
    1991   *Blessings of the Blood: A Book of Menstrual Lore and Rituals for Women* (Victoria, BC: Beach Holme).

Arnold, P.
    1992   *Wildmen, Warriors and Kings: Masculine Spirituality and the Bible* (New York: Crossroad).

Atkinson, C., M. Miles and C. Buchanan (eds.)
    1987   *Shaping New Vision: Gender and Values in American Culture* (Ann Arbor: University of Michigan Press).

Banks, O.
    1986   *Faces of Feminism: A Study of Feminism as a Social Movement* (Oxford: Basil Blackwell).

Beth, R.
    1990   *Hedgewitch* (London: Hale).

Billington, S., and M. Green (eds.)
    1996   *The Concept of the Goddess* (London: Routledge).

Binford, S.
    1982   'Myths and Matriarchies', in Spretnak (ed.), *The Politics of Women's Spirituality*.

Binford, S., C. Spretnak and M. Stone
    1982   'Are Goddesses and Matriarchies Merely Figments of Feminist Imagination?' in Spretnak (ed.), *The Politics of Women's Spirituality*.

Birnbaum, L.C.
    1993   *Black Madonnas: Feminism, Religion and Politics in Italy* (Boston: Northeastern University Press).

Bridle, S.
    1996   'Daughter of the Goddess: An Interview with Z. Budapest', *What is Enlightenment?* 5: 65-71.

Brooke, E.

1993   *A Woman's Book of Shadows: Witchcraft: A Celebration* (London: The
            Women's Press).

Budapest, Z.

1982   'The Vows, Wows, and Joys of the High Priestess or What do You
            People Do Anyway?', in Spretnak (ed.)1982.

1986   *The Holy Book of Women's Mysteries* (Oakland, CA: Wingbow Press).

1989   *The Grandmother of Time: A Woman's Book of Celebrations, Spells, and Sacred
            Objects for Every Month of the Year* (San Francisco: Harper & Row).

1992   'Self-Blessing Ritual', in Christ and Plaskow (eds.) 1992.

Burfield, D.

1983   'Theosophy and Feminism: Some Explorations in Nineteenth-Century
            Biography', in P. Holden (ed.), *Women's Religious Experience* (Beckenham,
            Kent: Croom Helm).

Cameron, A.

1989   'First Mother and the Rainbow Children', in Plant (ed.) 1989.

Caputi, J.

1993   *Gossips, Gorgons and Crones: The Fates of the Earth* (Santa Fe, NM: Bear &
            Co.).

Caron, C.

1996   'Thealogy' in L. Russell and J. Clarkson (eds.), *Dictionary of Feminist The-
            ologies* (London: Mowbray).

Chicago, J.

1982   'Our Heritage is Our Power', in Spretnak, (ed.) 1982.

Christ, C.P.

1978   'Heretics and Outsiders: The Struggle Over Female Power in Western
            Religion', *Soundings* 61: 260-280.

1983   'Symbols of Goddess and God in Feminist Theology', in Olson, (ed.)
            1993.

1987   *Laughter of Aphrodite* (New York: Harper & Row).

1988   'In Praise of Aphrodite: Sexuality as Sacred', in E. Dodson Gray (ed.),
            Sacred Dimensions of Women's Experience (Wellesley, MA: Roundtable
            Press).

1992   'Why Women Need the Goddess: Phenomenological, Psychological, and
            Political Reflections', in Christ and Plaskow (eds.) 1992.

1995   *Odyssey With the Goddess: A Spiritual Quest in Crete* (New York: Con-
            tinuum).

1997   *Rebirth of the Goddess: Finding Meaning in Feminist Spirituality* (Reading,
            MA: Addison–Wesley).

Christ, C.P., and J. Plaskow (eds.)

1992   *Womanspirit Rising: A Feminist Reader in Religion* (New York: Harper-
            SanFrancisco).

Clack, B.

1995   'The Denial of Dualism: Thealogical Reflections on the Sexual and the
            Spiritual', *Feminist Theology* 10: 102-15.

Clark, E., and H. Richardson (eds.)

1977   *Women and Religion: A Feminist Source Book of Christian Thought* (New
            York: Harper & Row).

Collins, S.
   1982   'The Personal is Political', in Spretnak (ed.) 1982.
Conway, D.J.
   1994   *Maiden, Mother, Crone: The Myth and Reality of the Triple Goddess* (St Paul, MN: Llewellyn).
Cranwell, C.
   1997   'Veganism and Feminist Eco-Paganism', *Wood and Water* 59: 4- 6.
Crowley, V.
   1995   'Wicca as a Modern-Day Mystery Religion', in Harvey and Hardman (ed.) 1995.
   1996   *Wicca: The Old Religion in the New Millennium* (London: Thorsons).
Culpepper, E.,
   1991   'The Spiritual, Political Journey of a Feminist Freethinker', in P. Cooey *et al.* (eds.), *After Patriarchy: Feminist Transformations of the World Religions* (Maryknoll, NY: Orbis Books).
   1997   'Contemporary Goddess Thealogy: A Sympathetic Critique', in Atkinson, Miles and Buchanan (eds.) 1987.
Daly, M.
   1975   'The Qualitative Leap Beyond Patriarchal Religion', *Quest: A Feminist Quarterly* 1: 20-40.
   1984   *Pure Lust: Elemental Feminist Philosophy* (London: The Women's Press)
   1985   *Beyond God the Father: Towards a Philosophy of Women's Liberation* (London: The Women's Press).
   1991   *Gyn/Ecology: The Metaethics of Radical Feminism* (London: The Women's Press).
   1993   *Outercourse: The Be-Dazzling Voyage* (London: The Women's Press).
Dames, M.
   1976   *Silbury Treasure: The Great Goddess Rediscovered* (London: Thames & Hudson).
Daum, A.
   1989   'Blaming the Jews for the Death of the Goddess', in E. Torton Beck (ed.), *Nice Jewish Girls: A Lesbian Anthology* (Boston: Beacon Press).
Davis, E. Gould
   1971   *The First Sex* (New York: Penguin Books).
Denise (no surname given)
   1993   'Out From Under the Skirts of Nature', *From the Flames* 9: 30-31.
Devaney, S.G.
   1995   In Roundtable Discussion, 'What's in a Name?', *Journal of Feminist Studies in Religion* 11: 119-23.
Dexter, M.R.
   1990   *Whence the Goddesses: A Sourcebook* (New York: Pergamon Press).
Diamond, I., and G. Orenstein (eds.)
   1990   *Reweaving the World: The Emergence of Ecofeminism* (San Francisco: Sierra Club Books).
Dinkelspiel, A.
   1981   'When the Sacred Canopy Rips Apart', *Journal of Women and Religion* 1: 2-6.

Douglas, M.
    1973   *Natural Symbols: Explorations in Cosmology* (London: Barrie & Jenkins).
Downing, C.
    1990   *The Goddess: Mythological Images of the Feminine* (New York: Crosroad).
Durkheim, E.
    1971   *Elementary Forms of the Religious Life* (repr. London: George Allen & Unwin).
Easton, C.
    1996   *Every Woman a Witch* (London: Quantum).
Ehrenreich, B., and D. English
    1972   *Witches, Midwives and Nurses* (New York: Glass Mountain).
Eilberg-Schwartz, H.
    1989   'Witches of the West: Neopaganism and Goddess Worship as Enlightenment Religions', *Journal of Feminist Studies in Religion* 5: 77-95.
Eisenstein, H.
    1984   *Contemporary Feminist Thought* (London: Unwin Paperbacks).
Eisler, R.
    1988   *The Chalice and the Blade: Our History, Our Future* (San Francisco: Harper & Row).
    1995a   'Envisioning a Partnership Future', *Woman of Power* 24: 20-27.
    1995b   *Sacred Pleasure: Sex, Myth and the Politics of the Body* (San Francisco: HarperSanFrancisco).
Eliade, M.
    1958   *Patterns in Comparative Religion* (London: Sheed & Ward).
    1965   *Rites and Symbols of Initiation: The Mysteries of Birth and Rebirth* (New York: Harper & Row).
Eller, C.
    1993   *Living in the Lap of the Goddess: The Feminist Spirituality Movement in America* (New York: Crossroad).
Ellice-Hopkins, J.
    1899   *The Power of Womanhood* (London: Wells, Gardner, Darton & Co.).
Estés, C.P.
    1992   *Women Who Run With the Wolves: Contacting the Power of the Wild Woman* (London: Rider).
Folz, T.G., and W. Griffin
    1996   '"She Changes Everything She Touches": Ethnographic Journeys of Self-Discovery', in C. Ellis and A.P. Bochner (eds.), *Composing Ethnography: Alternative Forms of Qualitative Writing* (Walnut Creek, CA: Altamira Press).
Francia, L.
    1991   *Dragontime: The Magic and Mystery of Menstruation* (Woodstock, NY: Ash Tree Publishing).
Gilligan, C.
    1982   *In a Different Voice: Psychological Theory and Women's Development* (Cambridge, MA: Harvard University Press).
Gimbutas, M.
    1982   'Women and Culture in Goddess Orientated Old Europe', in Spretnak (ed.) 1982.

1974   *The Goddesses and Gods of Old Europe 6500–3500 BC: Myths and Cult Images* (Berkeley: University of California Press).

Goldberg, N.
1990   *Wild Mind* (New York: Bantam).

Goldenberg, N.
1979   *Changing of the Gods: Feminism and the End of Traditional Religions* (Boston: Beacon Press).
1990   *Resurrecting the Body: Feminism, Religion, and Psychoanalysis* (New York: Crossroad).
1995   The Return of the Goddess: Psychoanalytic Reflections on the Shift from Theology to Thealogy', in King (ed.) 1995.

Göttner-Abendroth, H.
1991   *The Dancing Goddess: Principles of a Matriarchal Aesthetic* (Boston: Beacon Press).

Graham, E.
1995   *Making the Difference: Gender, Personhood and Theology* (London: Mowbray).

Green, M.
1991   *A Witch Alone* (Shaftesbury: Element).

Greenwood, S.
1995   'The Magical Will, Gender and Power in Magical Practices', in Harvey and Hardman (eds.) 1995.

Griffin, D.R. (ed.)
1988   *The Reenchantment of Science: Postmodern Proposals* (Albany, NY: State University of New York Press).

Griffin, S.
1978   *Woman and Nature: The Roaring Inside Her* (New York: Harper & Row).

Grigg, R.
1995   *When God Becomes Goddess: The Transformation of American Religion* (New York: Continuum).

Gross, R.
1986   'Suffering, Feminist Theory and Images of Goddess', *Anima* 13: 39-46.

Hackett, J.A.
1989   'Can a Sexist Model Liberate Us?: Ancient Near Eastern "Fertility" Goddesses', *Journal of Feminist Studies in Religion* 5: 65-76.

Hampson, D.
1990   *Theology and Feminism* (Oxford: Basil Blackwell).
1996   *After Christianity* (London: SCM Press).

Harvey, G.
1993   'Avalon from the Mists: The Contemporary Teaching of Goddess Spirituality', *Religion Today* 8: 10-13.
1996   'The Authority of Intimacy in Paganism and Goddess Spirituality', *Diskus* 4: 34-48.
1997   *Listening People: Speaking Earth: Contemporary Paganism* (London: Hurst & Co.).

Harvey, G., and C. Hardman (eds.)
1995   *Paganism Today* (London: Thorsons).

Hekman, S.J.
  1990   *Gender and Knowledge: Elements of a Postmodern Feminism* (Cambridge: Polity Press).
Holbrook, B.
  1983   'Menstrual Ritual' [for a girl's menarche] *WomanSpirit* 9: 36.
Husain, S. (ed.)
  1994   *The Virago Book of Witches* (London: Virago).
Iglehart, H.
           'The Unnatural Divorce of Spirituality and Politics', in Spretnak (ed.) 1992.
Jade (no surname given)
  1995   'The Six Paths of the Inner Mysteries: A Spiritual Leadership Program for Women', *Woman of Power* 24: 81-82.
Jaggar, A.
  1983   *Feminist Politics and Human Nature* (Brighton: Harvester).
Javors, I.
  1990   'The Goddess in the Metropolis: Reflections on the Sacred in an Urban Setting', in Diamond and Orenstein (eds.) 1990.
Jay, N.
  1991   'Gender and Dichotomy', in S. Gunew (ed.), *A Reader in Feminist Knowledge* (London: Routledge).
Jayran, S.
  1985   *Which Craft?: An Introduction to the Craft* (London: House of the Goddess).
  1994   *Circlework: A DIY Handbook for Working Ritual Psychology and Magic* (London: House of the Goddess).
  1995   *The Pagan Index (UK) 1995* (London: House of the Goddess).
  1997   'Introductory Notes: Goddess Thealogy', unpublished paper, given by the author.
Jean (no surname given)
  1993   'So this is the end of patriarchy?', *From the Flames* 11: 15-17.
Jeffreys, S.
  1985   *The Spinster and her Enemies: Feminism and Sexuality 1800–1930* (London: Pandora).
Joy, M.
  1995   'God and Gender: Some Reflections on Women's Invocations of the Divine', in King (ed.) 1995.
Keller, C.
  1988   'Goddess, Ear, and Metaphor: On the Journey of Nelle Morton', *Journal of Feminist Studies in Religion* 4: 51-67.
Kelly-Gadol, J.
  1983   'The Social Relation of the Sexes: Methodological Implications of Women's History' in E. Abel and E.K. Abel (eds.), *The Signs Reader: Women, Gender and Scholarship* (Chicago: University of Chicago Press).
King, L.
  1993   *A Whistling Woman is up to No Good: Finding Your Wild Woman* (Berkeley: Celestial Arts).
King, U.
  1989   *Women and Spirituality: Voices of Protest and Promise* (London: Macmillan).

King, U. (ed.)
    1995   *Religion and Gender* (Oxford: Basil Blackwell).
Koltuv, B.B.
    1986   *The Book of Lilith* (York Beach, ME: Nicolas-Hays).
LaPuma, K.
    1991   *Awakening Female Power: The Way of the Goddess Warrior* (Fairfax, CA: SoulSource).
Larrington, C. (ed.)
    1992   *The Feminist Companion to Mythology* (London: Pandora).
Lerner, G.
    1979   *The Majority Finds its Past: Placing Women in History* (New York: Oxford University Press).
Litwoman, J.
    1981   'Womon (sic) Identified Judaism', *WomanSpirit* 8: 40-41.
Long, A.
    1991   'Anti-Judaism in Britain', *Journal of Feminist Studies in Religion* 7: 125-33.s
    1994   'The Goddess Movement in Britain Today', *Feminist Theology* 5: 11-39.
    1996   Review of M. Raphael, *Thealogy and Embodiment* in *Wood and Water* 55: 14-15.
    1997   'The One or the Many: The Great Goddess Revisited', *Feminist Theology* 15: 13-29.
Luhrmann, T.
    1994   *Persuasions of the Witch's Craft: Ritual Magic in Contemporary England* (London: Macmillan).
Lunn, P.
    1993   'Do Women Need the GODDESS? Some Phenomenological and Sociological Reflections', *Feminist Theology* 4: 17-38.
MacIntyre, V.
    1993   'Making (a) Difference—Feminism, Diversity and Community', *From the Flames* 9: 32-34.
    1996   Review of M. Raphael, *Thealogy and Embodiment* in *From the Flames* 18: 36.
MacIntyre, V., *et al.*
    1993   'The End of Patriarchy. Extraordinary minutes of an extraordinary meeting on 10 January 1993 in Bristol', *From the Flames* 9: 3-5.
Macy, J.
    1983   'Taking Heart: Exercises for Activists', *WomanSpirit* 9: 54.
Madsen, C.
    1994   'A God of One's Own: Recent Work by and about Women in Religion', *Signs* 19: 480-98.
Malmgreen, G. (ed.)
    1986   *Religion in the Lives of English Women, 1760–1930* (London: Croom Helm).
Marler, J.
    1996   'The Life and Work of Marija Gimbutas', *Journal of Feminist Studies in Religion* 12: 37-47.
Marsden-McGlynn, C.
    1993   'Nudity', *The Deosil Dance* 36: 3-5.

Matthews, C.
    1989   *The Elements of The Goddess* (Shaftesbury: Element).
McCrickard, J.
    1991   'Born-Again Moon: Fundamentalism in Christianity and the Feminist
                Spirituality Movement', *Feminist Review* 37: 59-67.
McFague, S.
    1983   *Metaphorical Theology: Models of God in Religious Language* (London: SCM
                Press).
McPhillips, K.
    1994   'Women-Church and the Reclamation of Sacredness: A Response to Vic-
                toria Lee Erickson', *Journal of Feminist Studies in Religion* 10: 113-18.
Merchant, C.
    1980   *The Death of Nature* (San Francisco: Harper & Row).
    1990   'Ecofeminism and Feminist Theory', in Diamond and Orenstein (eds.)
                1990.
Millett, K.
    1972   *Sexual Politics* (London: Sphere).
Monaghan, P.
    1990   *The Book of Godesses and Heroines* (St Paul, MN: Llewellyn)
Morgan, R.
    1982   'WITCH: Spooking the Patriarchy during the Late Sixties', in Spretnak
                (ed.) 1992.
Moorey, T.
    1997   *The Goddess: A Beginner's Guide* (London: Headway).
Morton, N.
    1985   *The Journey is Home* (Boston: Beacon Press).
Murray, M.
    1921   *The Witch-Cult in Western Europe* (Oxford: Oxford University Press).
    1931   *God of the Witches* (New York: Oxford University Press).
Nicholson, L.J. (ed.)
    1990   *Feminism/Postmodernism* (London: Routledge).
Noddings, N.
    1984   *Caring: A Feminine Approach to Ethics and Moral Education* (Berkeley: Uni-
                versity of California Press).
Noble, V.
    1990   'Authorizing our Teachers: Teaching in a Spiritual Feminist Context',
                Woman of Power 24: 71-75.
Ochshorn, J.
    1981   *The Female Experience and the Nature of the Divine* (Bloomington: Indiana
                University Press).
Olson, C. (ed.)
    1983   *The Book of the Goddess Past and Present: An Introduction to her Religion*
                (New York: Crossroad).
Orenstein, Rabbi D. (ed.)
    1994   *Lifecycles: Jewish Women on Life Passages and Personal Milestones*, I (Wood-
                stock, VT: Jewish Lights Publishing).

Orenstein, G.
      1991   'Gender Politics and the Soul: A Jewish Feminist Journey', in Pirani (ed.),
                  The Absent Mother.
Ozaniec, N.
      1993   *Daughter of the Goddess: The Sacred Priestess* (London: Aquarian).
Pagan Federation, The
      1992   *Pagan Federation Information Pack* (London: The Pagan Federation),
      1993   *The Witchcraft Information Pack* (London: The Pagan Federation).
Pahnke, D.
      1995   'Religion and Magic in the Modern Cults of the Great Goddess', in King
                  (ed.) 1995: 165-76.
Paris, G.
      1992   *The Sacrament of Abortion* (Dallas: Spring Publications).
Patai, R.
      1967   *The Hebrew Goddess* (Detroit: Wayne State University Press).
Pirani, A.
      1991   'Creations of the Goddess', in *idem* (ed.) 1991.
Pirani, A. (ed.)
      1991   *The Absent Mother: Restoring the Goddess to Judaism and Christianity* (London: Mandala).
Plant, J. (ed.)
      1989   *Healing the Wounds: The Promise of Ecofeminism* (Philadelphia: New Society).
Plaskow, J.
      1991   *Standing Again at Sinai: Judaism from a Feminist Perspective* (New York: HarperCollins).
Plaskow, J., and C.P. Christ (eds.)
      1989   *Weaving the Visions: New Patterns in Feminist Theology* (New York: HarperSanFrancisco).
Read, D. (dir.)
      1989   *Goddess Remembered*, National Film Board of Canada.
      1990   *The Burning Times*, National Film Board of Canada.
      1992   *Full Circle*, Great Atlantic and Pacific Film Company and the National
                  Film Board of Canada.
Raphael, M.
      1995   '"Cover not our Blood with thy Silence": Sadism, Eschatological Justice
                  and Female Images of the Divine', *Feminist Theology* 8: 85-105.
      1996a   'J. Ellice Hopkins: The Construction of a Recent Spiritual Feminist
                  Foremother', *Feminist Theology* 13: 73-95.
      1996b   *Thealogy and Embodiment: The Post-Patriarchal Reconstruction of Female
                  Sacrality* (Sheffield: Sheffield Academic Press).
      1996c   'Truth in Flux: Goddess Feminism as a Late Modern Religion', *Religion*
                  26: 199-213.
      1997a   'Real-izing the Material: Spiritual Feminism and the Resacralization of the
                  Earth', in R. Carter and S. Eisenberg (eds.), *The Ideal in the World's
                  Religions: Essays on the Person, Family, Society and Environment* (St Paul,
                  Minnesota: Paragon Press).

1997b   'Thealogy, Redemption and the Call of the Wild', *Feminist Theology* 15: 55-72.

1998a   'Goddess Religion, Postmodern Jewish Feminism and the Complexity of Alternative Religious Identities', *Nova Religio* 1: 198-215.

1998b   'Thealogy and the Parthenogenetic Reproduction of Femaleness' in M. Hayes, W. Porter and D. Tombs (ed.), *Religion and Sexuality* (Sheffield: Sheffield Academic Press).

1999   'Monotheism in Contemporary Feminist Goddess Religion: A Betrayal of Early Thealogical Non-Realism?', in D. Sawyer and Diane Colliers (eds.), *From Isolation to Integration? New Directions in Feminist Theology* (Sheffield: Sheffield Academic Press).

Raschke, C.

1992   'Fire and Roses, or the Problem of Postmodern Religious Thinking', in P. Berry and A. Wernick (eds.), *Shadow of Spirit: Postmodernism and Religion* (London: Routledge).

Roney-Dougal, S.

1991   *Where Science and Magic Meet* (Shaftesbury: Element).

Rowan, J.

1987   *The Horned God: Feminism and Men as Wounding and Healing* (London: Routledge & Kegan Paul)

Ruddick, S.

1990   *Maternal Thinking: Towards a Politics of Peace* (London: The Women's Press).

Ruether, R.R.

1976   *New Woman/New Earth* (New York: Seabury Press).

1979   'A Religion for Women: Sources and Strategies', *Christianity and Crisis* 39: 307-11.

1980   Goddesses and Witches: Liberation and Countercultural Feminism', *The Christian Century* 94: 842-47.

1983   *Sexism and God-Talk: Towards a Feminist Theology* (London: SCM Press).

Sand, K.M.

1992   'Uses of the Thea(o)logian: Sex and Theodicy in Religious Feminism', *Journal of Feminist Studies in Religion* 8: 7-33.

Scott, N.

1971   *The Wild Prayer of Longing* (New Haven: Yale University Press).

Shepsut A.

1993   *Journey of the Priestess: The Priestess Traditions of the Ancient World* (London: Aquarian).

Sjöö, M.

1992   *New Age and Armageddon: The Goddesses or the Gurus? Towards a Feminist Vision of the Future* (London: The Women's Press).

1993   'Breaking the Tabu—Doing the Unthinkable', *From the Flames* 10: 22-23.

1994   'International Women's Day . . . And Women Priests', *From the Flames* 13: 15-16.

Sjöö, M., and B. Mor

1991   *The Great Cosmic Mother: Rediscovering the Religion of the Earth* (New York: HarperSanFrancisco).

Smart, N.

    1996   *Dimensions of the Sacred: An Anatomy of the World's Beliefs* (London: Harper Collins).

Spretnak, C. (ed.)

    1982   *The Politics of Women's Spirituality: Essays on the Rise of Spiritual Power Within the Feminist Movement* (New York: Anchor Books).

    1990   'Ecofeminism: Our Roots and Flowering', in Diamond and Orenstein (eds.) 1990.

    1992   *Lost Goddesses of Early Greece: A Collection of Pre-Hellenic Myths* (Boston: Beacon Press).

Spretnak, C., and F. Capra

    1985   *Green Politics: The Global Promise* (London: Paladin)

Starhawk

    1979   *The Spiral Dance: A Rebirth of the Religion of the Great Goddess* (New York: Harper & Row).

    1982a   'Ethics and Justice in Goddess Religion', in Spretnak (ed.) 1982.

    1982b   'Witchcraft as Goddess Religion', in Spretnak (ed.) 1982.

    1987   *Truth or Dare: Encounters with Power, Authority and Mystery* (New York: HarperSanFrancisco).

    1989a   'Feminism, Earth-Based Spirituality and Ecofeminism', in Plant (ed.) 1989: 174-85.

    1989b   In Roundtable Discussion, 'If God is God She is not Nice', *Journal of Feminist Studies in Religion* 5: 105-106.

    1990a   *Dreaming the Dark: Magic, Sex and Politics* (London: Mandala).

    1990b   'Power, Authority and Mystery: Ecofeminism and Earth-Based Spirituality', in Diamond and Orenstein (eds.) 1990.

    1992   'Witchcraft and Women's Culture', in Christ and Plaskow (eds.) 1992.

    1994   *The Fifth Sacred Thing* (New York: Bantam).

    1995   'A New Political Agenda', reprinted in *Wood and Water* 55 (1996): 2-7.

    1997   *Walking to Mercury* (London: Thorsons).

Stein, D.

    1993   *Stroking the Python: Women's Psychic Lives* (St Paul, MN: Llewellyn).

Stone, M.

    1976   *When God was a Woman* (New York).

    1991   *Ancient Mirrors of Womanhood* (Boston: Beacon Press).

Straffon, C.

    1994   'Pagan Philosophy and Women', *From the Flames* 13: 26-27.

Tate, K.

    1997b   'Behold, I Have Been With You Since the Beginning: A Woman Finds the Goddess', *Wood and Water* 60: 7-8.

    1997a   'The Goddess in Greece', *Wood and Water* 58: 2-4.

Teubal, S.

    1984   *Sarah the Priestess: The First Matriarch of Genesis* (Athens, Ohio: First Swallow Press/Ohio Univerisity Press).

Tong, R.

    1992   *Feminist Thought: A Comprehensive Introduction* (London: Routledge).

Townsend, J.
    1990   'The Goddess: Fact, Fallacy and Revitalization Movement', in L.W. Hurtado (ed.), *Goddesses in Religion and Modern Debate* (Atlanta: Scholars Press).

Walker, B.
    1983   *The Woman's Encyclopedia of Myths and Secrets* (New York: HarperSanFrancisco).
    1988   *The Crone: Woman of Age, Wisdom and Power* (New York: Harper Collins).

Weaver, M.-J.
    1989   'Who is the Goddess and Where Does She Get Us?', *Journal of Feminist Studies in Religion* 5: 49-64.

Weinstein, M.
    1978   *Positive Magic* (Custer, WA: Phoenix).
    1986   *Earth Magic* (Custer, WA: Phoenix).

West, A.
    1995   *Deadly Innocence: Feminism and the Mythology of Sin* (London: Cassell).

Wilshire, D.
    1994   *Virgin, Mother, Crone: Myths and Mysteries of the Triple Goddess* (Rochester, VT: Inner Traditions).

Wollstonecraft, M.
    1975   *Vindication of the Rights of Women* (ed. C.H. Poston; New York: W.W. Norton).

Woodhead, L.
    1993   'Post-Christian Spiritualities', *Religion* 23: 167-81.

Young, S. (ed.)
    1993   *An Anthology of Sacred Texts By and About Women* (London: Pandora).

INDEX OF AUTHORS